"... some
that
trouble
you ..."

"...some that trouble you..."

SUBCULTURES IN MORMONISM

CLAIR L. WYATT

BOOKCRAFT INC.
SALT LAKE CITY, UTAH

Library of Congress Catalog Card Number: 74-75167

ISBN 0-88494-209-0

1st Printing, 1974

LITHOGRAPHED IN U.S.A.

PUBLISHERS PRESS
SALT LAKE CITY, UTAH

I marvel that ye are so soon removed from him that called you into the grace of Christ unto another gospel:

Which is not another; but there be some that trouble you, and would pervert the gospel of Christ.

—Galatians 1:6-7.

Contents

Preface

In recent years the Authorities of The Church of Jesus Christ of Latter-day Saints have said very little about the various Fundamentalist cult groups. This is as it should be; a campaign to answer the cultists would only divert the Church from its important work of the kingdom, focus attention upon and provide free publicity for their movements, and perhaps appear to give some credibility to these movements. However, when one discovers that close relatives have become involved, it is difficult to ignore the problem. The involvement progresses from criticism of Church leadership to loss of Church membership. Finally, when children are born to illegal, so-called plural marriages, relatives find their very heart strings broken and trampled, their families disrupted, and their relationships strained.

The cultist system of theology is seemingly rational, and most of their beliefs are so nearly identical to accepted Church doctrine that the uninitiated person feels helpless to counter their position. The question of Fundamentalism has the appearance of being extremely complex and involved.

After having close relatives become involved in cultism, I again had to confront this problem as a bishop when members of my ward became deeply involved in it. Once again, I observed frustration, sorrow, and a feeling of helplessness on the part of bewildered relatives. The writing of this work is in direct response to these challenges and personal experiences.

As will be seen, I have developed a broad view of the cultist syndrome to find common factors of motivation, relationship to contemporary society, and the means to obtain practical goals among various cult groups in history. I have also determined the real issue, which is the grounds or premise upon which contemporary Fundamentalist cult theology is based. The whole message of this writing is to reaffirm that "the true people of God in all ages are founded upon that kind of revelation that comes only through living prophets" while the cult movements are all "founded upon alleged priesthood provisions given in secret to men who are all dead and who left no testimonies of these events as required by the law of witnesses."

The object of this work is to set forth the doctrine of prophetic revelation as being in direct opposition to the cult beliefs and practices, and to make it impossible for anyone to confuse cultism with The Church of Jesus Christ of Latter-day Saints.

Since the research upon which this book is based took place over a number of years, I am indebted to many persons. In particular I wish to express appreciation to Mrs. Marleen Hirschi, who did most of the typing, and to Mrs. Patricia Braegger and my wife Carolyn for critically reading the book and making many valuable suggestions. However, I must take full responsibility for the contents.

Chapter One

Challenge and Conflict

Introduction

Throughout history, and over widespread areas of the earth, various groups have maintained their own systems of belief and practice within a surrounding pluralistic and complex society. Every system is challenged directly or indirectly by other systems. Our present society in America is founded upon revolution against authority, as were most former systems. As we look back through the annals of time, we see wave after wave of change sweeping men's minds from one system to another.

In the midst of a sea of challenge and conflict we may well ask: "What is to be done? Who of all these parties are right; or, are they all wrong together?"[1] The Prophet Joseph Smith asked these questions and, as a result, The Church of Jesus Christ of Latter-day Saints was organized in the state of New York on April 6, 1830.

During the more than 140 years that have elapsed since the Church was organized in 1830, there have been numerous splinter groups[2] formed by dissident followers of the Prophet

---

[1]Joseph Smith 2:10.

[2]Lyle O. Wright, "Origins and Development of the Church of the Firstborn of the Fulness of Times," (Provo: unpublished Ph.D. dissertation, Brigham Young University, 1963). This work presents an excellent historical development of numerous spurious claims to authority made by dissenters from The Church of Jesus Christ of Latter-day Saints.

Joseph Smith. Each of these dissident groups claims to possess the truth and attempts to substantiate that claim through supernatural experiences.

Subcultures

These dissident groups often take the form of a subculture, which is a group that exhibits characteristic social patterns of behavior sufficient to distinguish it from others within an embracing culture of society.

Orthodox Mormonism may be classified as a subculture in America. This was particularly so during the middle and late nineteenth century when Mormonism exhibited characteristic social patterns of behavior distinctly different from the surrounding American society. The practice of gathering and the associated cooperative living,[3] and the practice of plural marriage or polygamy were major social characteristics that played a heavy role in the persecution of members of the Church.

Toward the end of the nineteenth century, the Mormons became well established in the Intermountain regions of the United States. Political, social, and economic pressures eventually brought about a gradual end to the cooperative principle and monolithic character of Mormon society. Although these cooperative practices served well in carving a viable and industrious society out of the wilderness,[4] they were out of step with twentieth-century American economics.

The practice of polygamy also was discontinued in 1890 when the president of the Church, Wilford Woodruff, issued the Manifesto[5] calling a halt to the contracting of all polygamous marriages thoughout the world.

---

[3]*Deseret News,* June 2, 1869. Brigham Young in a sermon of April 7, 1869, declared, "This cooperative movement is only a stepping stone to what is called the *Order of Enoch,* but what is in reality the *Order of Heaven."* The *Order of Enoch,* sometimes referred to as the *United Order* or the *Law of Consecration,* is so-called because of a description of Enoch and his people. "And the Lord called his people Zion, because they were of one heart and one mind, and dwelt in righteousness; and there was no poor among them." (Moses 7:18.)

[4]Thomas F. O'Dea, *The Mormons* (Chicago: The University of Chicago Press, 1957), pp. 199-200.

[5]D&C, "Official Declaration," p. 256.

Thus, after 1890, with the end of the cooperative principle and the practice of polygamy, the most distinctive social characteristics of Mormonism disappeared and the Utah-based Mormon culture moved ever closer to the mainstream of American life.[6] Virtually all significant political opposition to Mormonism had disappeared by the middle of the twentieth century.

While the Church discontinued the social practice of gathering and cooperative living, and the practice of polygamy, its official position is that these are correct principles.[7] However, these principles may be properly practiced only when they serve a social need and are commanded and authorized by God through revelation to his living prophets. Bruce R. McConkie declares the principle of plural marriage is a necessary part of the restitution of all things, and an ennobling and exalting principle when authorized by the Lord, but not essential to salvation or exaltation.[8] This is illustrated in the case of the Nephites, who were commanded, "For there shall not any man among you have save it be one wife; and concubines he shall have none."[9] This was a countercommand to that given to the forefathers of the Nephites: namely, Abraham, Isaac, and Jacob. Yet the Nephites could gain every blessing in eternity that God ever promised any people.

Mormon Subcultures

Most of the Mormon splinter groups that have formed since the organization of the Church can be classified under two major headings: those that were opposed to the *principle* and *practice* of plural marriage and gathering, and those that were opposed to the *discontinuation* of the *practice* of these principles. These groups profess allegiance to Joseph Smith as a true prophet of God, and to the Book of Mormon as being

---

[6]Leonard J. Arrington, *Great Basin Kingdom* (Lincoln: University of Nebraska Press, 1966), p. 352.

[7]Bruce R. McConkie, *Mormon Doctrine* (Salt Lake City: Bookcraft, 1966), p. 578.

[8]Ibid., p. 577.

[9]Jacob 2:27.

divinely inspired, and so claim to be recognized as part of Mormonism.

The earliest splinter groups were composed of persons left behind as the body of the Church moved from New York to Ohio, Missouri, Illinois, and finally to the West. Each of these moves was associated with great persecution and bloodshed. These individuals found freedom from the persecution that the main body was subjected to by remaining dispersed. They lacked either the disposition or wherewithal to move west. In effect, they rejected the gathering and Zion-building concept; and they emphatically rejected polygamy, whose introduction they attributed to Brigham Young and others.[10] These people wanted a more conventional religion based, as they viewed it, upon Joseph Smith, the Book of Mormon, and a Protestant type of religious-social life. This they found in the Reorganized Church of Jesus Christ of Latter Day Saints into which many were unified some years after the great Mormon exodus to the West.[11]

The discontinuation of the practice of plural wives in 1890 gave rise to the later schism resulting in the formation of various cult groups. These groups are referred to as *Fundamentalists*. This term, as they use it, designates a return to or retention of the pre-Manifesto practices of the Church; namely, polygamy, the cooperative principle and other doctrines.

The members of these groups often work inside the main church as regular members. The Fundamentalist teachings are so subtle and seemingly so "Mormon" as to deceive many orthodox; the cult practices are sometimes hidden within a complex web of secrecy and deception. When individuals are exposed and excommunicated from the Church for cult prac-

---

[10]Richard P. Howard, "The Reorganized Church in Illinois, 1852-82 Search for Identity," *Dialogue,* 5 (Spring 1966), pp. 66-68. There was, in addition to the polygamy question, a closely associated question of leadership — namely, who should succeed the Prophet Joseph Smith — and a clear rejection of those who, like Brigham Young, advocated polygamy.

[11]Ibid., p. 63.

tices, they often band together in various communal enclaves from Mexico to Montana.[12]

Although Fundamentalist groups reject current Church leadership regarding plural marriage, communal living, and other doctrines, many of them continue to regard themselves as members of The Church of Jesus Christ of Latter-day Saints, which they declare to be the only true Church, and they also declare its prophet to be God's prophet. They look forward to the day when the Church will be set straight by "one mighty and strong." Generally this is interpreted to mean the Prophet Joseph Smith returned from the dead;[13] however, others of the cultists claim to be the "one mighty and strong" or they anticipate his early appearance.[14] The Fundamentalist cult groups are a source of embarrassment to the Church, which considers them heretical.

The object of this book is to describe the origin, history, theology, and current practices of these polygamous cult groups; to demonstrate by history, reasoning, and scripture the error of their position; to set forth the doctrine of prophetic revelation as being in direct opposition to their beliefs; and to make it impossible for anyone to confuse modern polygamy cultism with The Church of Jesus Christ of Latter-day Saints.

---

[12]*Ravalli Republican,* June 19, 1972. George Danker and Bob Gilluly describe the "Pinesdale Community Based on Religion, Free Governing."

[13]Norman C. Pierce, *The 3½ Years* (No publishing details imprinted, 1963), p. 95.

[14]Wright, *Origins,* pp. 27-50.

Chapter Two

Historical Comparisons

Introduction

It is the purpose of this chapter to place the Mormon subcultures in their proper historical setting. It will be shown that they are not unique but, in fact, are typical of a long procession of groups exhibiting similar characteristics. In light of their predecessors, the cult groups will not seem so strange. Indeed, it will be shown that the characteristics they hold in common are more abundant than their differences. Particularly is this true of their relationship to contemporary society, factors of motivation, and practical means used to achieve goals.

From the earliest recorded times down to the present, various groups of individuals have rejected their contemporary society, declaring it to be corrupt and decadent, and have subsequently gone out into the wilderness, literally or figuratively speaking, where they have attempted to achieve a norm of perfection through some form of communal living and other practices. Often there has been a certain tyranny of the majority associated with established society, the struggle to keep up with the "rat race," and a hand-me-down culture. It may cause people to want to drop out of society when they find that life is too complex and has too many grey areas. They seek an idealism that portrays life in black and white terms; and they try to create an enclave of perfection.[1]

---

[1]Wallace E. Stegner, "Variations on a Theme of Dissent" (Logan: Utah State University Commencement Address, June 3, 1972).

The Essenes

An interesting community is the one that produced the famous Dead Sea Scrolls. The ruins of this community and the caves that held the documents lie in the forbidding ravine of Qumran, at the northern end of the Dead Sea. The prevailing view of scholars is that the people of Qumran were Essenes, a religious brotherhood described by the first-century writers Philo and Josephus.[2] Coins collected in the ruins indicated that they were inhabited more or less continuously from 125 B.C. to A.D. 68.

The primary source of information concerning the basic principles and practices of the people of the scrolls is the *Book of Order* or *Manual of Discipline*. The community's main purpose was "to exemplify and promulgate the true interpretation. It bases that interpretation on a kind of 'apostolic succession' begun by the prophets and continued by a series of inspired leaders."[3]

These "covenanters" ate and drank at common meals. They did not own private property, but upon admission to the sect did sell all they possessed and gave the price to the common fund. The members of the community described themselves as the "Elect of God" and "Sons of Light." Their basic tenet was that they constituted the true remnant of Israel.

Thus, in the case of the people of Qumran, they considered their contemporary society to be in a state of partial or perhaps total apostasy; they considered themselves as bearers of the prophetic truths which, in absence of contemporary prophecy, were guarded and perpetuated by a series of inspired group leaders; they had created an enclave, a refuge within which they could strive for perfection by the strictest adherence to the rule of the discipline; they could visualize themselves as the elect of God, commissioned by him to guard and perpetuate a body of knowledge which only they possessed.

---

[2]Frank Moore Cross, Jr., *The Ancient Library of Qumran* (Garden City, New York: Anchor Books, 1961), pp. 51-68.

[3]Theodor H. Gaster, *The Dead Sea Scriptures* (Garden City, New York: Anchor Books, 1964), p. 6.

Asceticism

The ancient Greeks and the Christians who adopted Greek philosophy and practice into their religion gave rise to various other groups. Both Greeks and Christians practiced asceticism. The Greek word from which *asceticism* is derived means practice or training for the attainment of an ideal. In Christianity, asceticism took on many forms, but often was conceived as a means to obtain perfection and as a gateway to mysticism.[4]

Many of the religious orders of the Catholic Church practice asceticism, providing a retreat from the complexities and anxieties of society into a simple communal life where perfection is visualized in terms of strict adherence to the rules of the order. Those known as the *contemplative* or *enclosed* orders provide a life completely cut off from the outside world. It is contended that it is the contemplatives that are at the heart of Christianity. They, not those who serve mankind, provide the greatest contribution to humanity through their intimate contact with God. Thus, these ascetic orders of the Catholic Church have created an enclave, a refuge from the world, and a discipline of perfection.

Amish or Plain People

The Protestant movement was not without examples of cult groups. The group known as the *Amish* or plain people is one. This movement originated in Zurich, Switzerland, in the early sixteenth century.[5] Its founders were contemporaries of Luther and Zwingli. They objected to baptism of infants and so were referred to as Anabaptists or Mennonites. They went far beyond Luther or Zwingli in rejecting Catholic theology and practice, suffering great persecutions and having many martyrs well into the seventeenth century. Many schisms occurred in the Mennonite movement. The full name of the Amish is *Old Order Amish Mennonite*. They are centered in Pennsylvania, Ohio, and Indiana. These people try to preserve the simple life of their Swiss ancestors of the

[4]*Encyclopedia Britannica*, 2 (1969), 561.

[5]John C. Wenger, *Glimpses of Mennonite History and Doctrine* (Scottdale, Pennsylvania: Herald Press, 1959), 258 pages.

seventeenth century. They oppose any innovations. The Amish people wear dark clothing. The men wear beards and broad-brimmed hats and the women wear long dresses and rimless bonnets.

The Amish people use horses and buggies, have simple homes, no indoor plumbing, electric lights, or telephones. However, they are good farmers and hard workers. Church services are held in their homes and they build no church buildings. Their religious philosophy is based upon a literal interpretation of the scriptures and justification by faith. Thus, the Amish avoid the complexities of a rapidly changing society and attempt to shield their children from a "wicked world"by retreating into the seventeenth century.

Gnostics

Perhaps the most striking parallel to the Mormon polygamy cult groups is found in the second-century Gnostics. Eusebius reports that "the enemy of all truth" was devising new methods to fight the Church. Having been cut off from his "former persecutions," he was now employing wicked impostors as instruments of destruction. "He instigated these insidious impostors and deceivers, by assuming the same name with us [Christians], to lead those believers whom they happen to seduce to the depths of destruction."[6] Thus the members of this heretical sect were posing as members of the Church and their teachings were similar enough to those of the Church to deceive many.

The word *gnosis* is Greek for knowledge. The Gnostics claimed that they had the *gnosis* (revealed knowledge), the secret things the Lord taught to Peter, James, and John after the resurrection. The ancient historian Irenaeus' one and only surviving work, written between A.D. 182 and 188, is entitled *Refutation and Overthrow of False Doctrine*[7] or *A Refutation and Subversion of Knowledge Falsely So-Called.*[8]

---

[6]Eusebius Pamphilus, *The Eccleseastical History* (London: George Bell & Sons, 1876), Book 4, chapter 7, p. 121.

[7]Ibid., Book 5, chapter 7, p. 174.

[8]"Irenaeus Against Heresies," in *The Anti-Nicene Fathers* (Grand Rapids, Michigan: Eerdmans Publishing Co., 1953), Introductory Note, p. 313.

There was a true gnosis, certain knowledge, entrusted to the Authorities of the Church after the resurrection and, so far as is known, to no one else. This is confirmed by Eusebius as he quotes Clement, "The Lord imparted the gift of knowledge [gnosis] to James the Just, to John, and Peter after his resurrection, these delivered it to the rest of the apostles, and they to the seventy, of whom Barnabas was one."[9] It has been suggested[10] that this knowledge imparted by the Lord to his Church Authorities after his death and resurrection consisted of the *endowment* and associated ordinances of the Melchizedek Priesthood.[11] This knowledge in all ages has been restricted to those who prove themselves worthy and who are willing to consecrate themselves to the building up of the Church and kingdom.

The first men to write against the Gnostics were always careful to designate them as the pretended Gnostics and their teachings as the false knowledge.[12] The Gnostics worked inside the Church as regular members and their teachings were "craftily decked out in an attractive dress, so as, by its outward form to make it appear . . . more true than truth itself."[13] These supposed truths include "knowledge of the Father,—namely, that he cannot be understood or comprehended, nor so much as seen or heard, except in so far as he is known by the Monogenes [Gnostics] only."[14] "They tell us, however, that this knowledge has not been openly divulged, because all are not capable of receiving it."[15]

The Gnostics had many teachings that carried an air of mystery and that implied superior knowledge. They felt that the true nature of God was beyond the grasp of ordinary Christians. They claimed prophetic powers, supernatural experiences; they brought forth faked but sensational apocryphal

---

[9]Eusebius, *History,* Book 2, chapter 1, p. 37.

[10]Hugh Nibley, *Since Cumorah* (Salt Lake City: Deseret Book Company, 1970), p. 114.

[11]D&C 84:19-22; 95:8.

[12]Irenaeus, *Anti-Nicene Fathers,* Book 1, Preface: 1.

[13]Ibid., Book 1, Preface: 2.

[14]Ibid., Book 1, 2:5.

[15]Ibid., Book 1, 3:1.

writings; they produced a ridiculous imitation of baptism and even celestial marriage; and they justified illegal and immoral sexual relationships between certain of their elite.

> Wherefore also it comes to pass, that the "most perfect" among them addict themselves without fear to all kinds of forbidden deeds of which the scriptures assure us that "they who do such things shall not inherit the kingdom of God." . . . Some of them, moreover, are in the habit of defiling these women to whom they have taught the above doctrine . . . they are in the habit of using these very words "whosoever being in this world does not so love a woman as to obtain possession of her, is not of the truth."[16]

The above, all from Irenaeus, might apply equally well today if the word *Fundamentalist* were substituted for *Gnostics* and *Mormon* for *Christian*. The similarity of the claims, the perversions, and the relationships to the Church is remarkable.

After making the claim that they possessed the revealed gnosis, the Gnostics had to verify that claim through supernatural experiences, particularly prophecy. At this they failed miserably, as recorded by Eusebius in the case of a prophecy concerning an impending general war that was to follow the death of the Lady Maximilla.[17] They, therefore, fell back on mysticism which was deep and mysterious enough to satisfy them as a substitute for prophetic revelation. Thus, the Gnostic movement constituted a schism within the primitive Church like the Fundamentalist schism in the modern Church. Both claimed to have exclusive knowledge, worked within the Church, and claimed mystic confirmation of their position.

Conclusion

In modern times, and particularly in America where freedom permits, revolution is a way of life. The Maoists, Venceremos, drug cults, Hippies and Yippies drop out of society, each seeking a simpler life.

Many people yearn for peaceful simplicity, and their experimentation toward the perfected society is an attempt to

---

[16]Ibid., Book 1, 6:3-4.

[17]Eusebius, *History*, Book 5, chapter 16, p. 186.

escape the complexities of society. They find an attractiveness in systems that do not call for constant choice. People who drop out of society are feeling this attraction. The drug-culture people feel it; so did the people of Qumran, the Ascetics, the Mennonites, and the Mormon cult groups. The rich young man who came to the Christ felt it as he asked, "What shall I do to inherit eternal life?" and when he heard Jesus' answer, "he was very sorrowful." Rather than some *one* thing that would give him the immediate assurance of perfection, he was told that he must give and serve and follow Christ.[18]

These examples, limited as they are in scope, may serve to provide the cardinal points that can serve to guide us somewhat when examining any subculture. No attempt has been made thus far to give a *right* or *wrong* evaluation of these various movements; but when it becomes necessary to make such decisions, it will be extremely helpful to understand those factors that are common in such groups. They are first a rejection of contemporary society, and second an attempt to gain perfection—these are the cardinal points. These points give rise to other factors that are inevitably present: claims to exclusive knowledge, opportunity for rank and honor in the system, a cause to which persons can associate themselves, and a simplistic outlook on life that eliminates many of the shady areas and frustrations of life.

---

[18]Luke 18:18-23.

Chapter Three

Cult Motivation

Introduction

The Viennese psychotherapist, Dr. Victor Frankl, stated that "man's search for meaning is a primary force in his life" and many persons complain of the "feeling of the total and ultimate meaninglessness of their lives. They lack the awareness of a meaning worth living for. They are haunted by the experience of their inner emptiness, a void within themselves; they are caught in that situation which I have called the 'existential vacuum'."[1]

Man's need for meaning is as basic a drive as sex or hunger. When a person is deprived by the skepticism of his culture of confidence in any ultimate values, he desperately seeks a substitute. Man in the existential vacuum may try to make meaning out of the accumulation of material things, he may substitute sex adventure and sensationalism for meaning, or simply try to drown his anxieties in alcohol. None of these substitutes works for long. The inhabitant of the existential vacuum finds himself shuttling between periods of hyperactivity and extreme despondency.

Victor Frankl stated, "I doubt whether a doctor can answer this question [the meaning of life] in general terms. For the meaning of life differs from man to man."[2] "What man

[1]Victor E. Frankl, *Man's Search for Meaning* (New York: Washington Square Press, 1963), pp. 154, 167.

[2]Ibid., p. 171.

actually needs is not a tensionless state but rather the striving, a struggling for some goal worthy of him."[3]

We have here the required elements to provide meaning to life: a goal or cause worth making a sacrifice to achieve; a journey to make, a mission to fulfill, a calling to answer. History is full of examples of dedicated men who were able to find fulfillment for their lives, some for good purposes and some for evil purposes. It is ironic indeed that these life-meaning needs can be fulfilled in numerous and opposing systems.

John Locke, in his "Essay Concerning Human Understanding" suggested this dilemma when he attempted to set down the "*grounds* [premise or foundation] of those persuasions which are to be found amongst men." He noted that these persuasions are so different and so opposing and yet are "asserted somewhere or other with such assurance and confidence" that a person who might observe this opposition and devotion might come to the conclusion that "there is no such thing as truth at all or that mankind" has no means to obtain a knowledge of the truth.[4]

These observations lead to the conclusion that a persuasion or system may satisfy man's need for meaning in life, but the fact that a given system can fulfill these needs cannot be construed as proof or even evidence that the system is based upon truth or is in the best good. In fact, some systems that have extracted the greatest of diligent service on the part of individuals and even of whole nations have been directed toward evil designs. It is only necessary to look at the great wars and the associated dedication of the military and patriotism of the citizenry on both sides to establish that unhappy fact.

It is also ironic that extremist groups that seek to create a perfect society, groups whose activities are in opposition to the embracing culture, are far better equipped to supply these life-meaning needs than middle-of-the-road cultures. This is

---

[3]Ibid., p. 166.

[4]John Locke, "An Essay Concerning Human Understanding," in *Great Books of the Western World,* 54 vols. (Chicago: William Benton, Publisher—Encyclopedia Britannica, Inc., 1952), 35:93. (Italics added.)

because they provide an escape from the apathy of the times and they thrive on persecution.

The cultist benefits in three ways to escape the existential vacuum: first, he can become associated with a great *cause;* second, he gains a unique comradeship or *brotherhood* with those who share his dedication to the cause: third, he has opportunity to gain *rank* and express himself in a leadership position within the movement, which builds within him a feeling of self-importance and worth.

That these needs can be supplied by opposing systems is illustrated in the following examples of the Communist Party in America in the post-World-War-Two years, and the Mormon Fundamentalist cult groups. The first, the Communist Party, is a godless atheistic system; while the second, the Fundamentalist, is diametrically opposite, having a claimed deeply religious ground or premise.

Communist Party

During the 1950s, intelligent and educated men, reared in America and familiar with the democratic way of life, joined the underground Communist Party in America. Such was the case with Alger Hiss, Whittaker Chambers, the Rosenbergs who gave Russia the secrets of the atomic bomb, and others who dedicated their lives to the Communist Party and betrayed their native land.[5]

There can be no doubt that the Communist movement of the fifties provided a *cause* for which these men would risk their lives and fortunes. The Communists promised the three things that the common man of the world, the worker, almost always had been denied: land, food, and peace. The elimination of war and poverty has been the dream of mankind since Cain slew Abel. No one can argue against such goals, but the ruthless and freedom-depriving means used by the Communists in their attempt to achieve such ends are totally unacceptable.

---

[5]W. Cleon Skousen, *The Naked Communist* (Salt Lake City: The Ensign Publishing Company, 1961), pp. 141, 144, 200.

The Communist Party was illegal in the United States during those years, so it was forced to operate underground. Thus, members of the Party experienced a unique *comradeship* that always exists between members of a persecuted minority. They were by necessity forced to devise conspiratorial plots that bound them together by oaths, covenants, and secrecy.

Finally, the Party apparatus provided opportunity for the diligent worker to gain *rank,* to move up in the organization. The opportunity to exercise leadership and obtain respect and honor from party members satisfied the need to feel important and worth while.

Fundamentalist Groups

The Fundamentalist *cause* is usually stated, "It is better to obey God than it is to obey man," which has reference primarily to the practice of "the Most Holy Principle," or just "the Principle," as the practice of plural marriage is referred to by the Fundamentalists.[6] The principle was first revealed to the Prophet Joseph Smith and was declared by Heber C. Kimball to be "one of the most holy principles that God ever revealed to man."[7] Brigham Young stated, as pertaining to that day and time when plural marriage was the Lord's law:

> The only men who become Gods, even the Sons of God are those who enter into polygamy. Others attain unto a glory and may even be permitted to come unto the presence of the Father and the Son, but they cannot reign as Kings in Glory, because they had blessings offered them and they refused to accept them.[8]

As was indicated in chapter 1 concerning the Nephites, those who have lived at times when the principle of plural marriage was not operative will not on that account be prevented from obtaining the highest rewards in the hereafter.

---

[6]Anonymous, *The Most Holy Principle, the Law and Testimony,* 3 vols. (Murray, Utah: Gems Publishing Company, 1970).

[7]Brigham Young and others, *Journal of Discourses,* 26 vols. (Liverpool, England: 1854-1886), 11:211.

[8]*Journal of Discourses,* 11:269.

The first congressional act against the practice of plural marriage was the Morrill Act of 1862. This act was declared constitutional by the U.S. Supreme Court in 1879. In the year 1882 the Edmunds-Tucker Bill was enacted, which became law in 1887, disincorporating the Church, escheating its property, and imposing other indignities. Many of the leading brethren of the Church served prison terms rather than give up their wives and families; others went into hiding.

In 1884, President John Taylor ordered an end to the sealing of plural marriages in the temples and the movement went underground. During that period, after having obtained their endowments in the temple, those desiring to be sealed in a plural marriage traveled to Canada or Mexico, where those marriages could be performed without breaking the laws of the United States.

In 1890, President Wilford Woodruff issued the Manifesto, bringing a stop to plural marriages on a worldwide basis. However, the underground movement continued, some claiming a special revelation to John Taylor in 1886 which relieved the Church of responsibility in this matter and placed it upon the individual, and authorized the performing of such marriages.[9] Finally, in 1904, President Joseph F. Smith reaffirmed the worldwide application of the Manifesto and declared that any member of the Church solemnizing or entering into such plural marriages "will be deemed in transgression against the church and will be liable to be dealt with according to the rules and regulations thereof, and excommunicated therefrom."[10]

Thus, since these declarations, the Fundamentalists have not only felt the wrath of the government but have also been ostracized by the Church. As with the Communist movement in the fifties, the Fundamentalist movement is illegal and therefore must operate underground. The members of the underground Fundamentalist groups, like members of the under-

[9]Joseph W. Musser, *The Four Hidden Revelations* (No publishing details imprinted), p. 24.

[10]Joseph F. Smith in *Conference Report of The Church of Jesus Christ of Latter-day Saints,* April 1904, p. 75.

ground Communist Party of the 1950s, were able to derive the same life-meaning needs of cause, brotherhood, and rank. They, like the Communists, are forced to devise conspiratorial plots to hide their actions from the Church, from opposing family members and associates, and from the government. Thus, they bind themselves together by oaths, covenants, and secrecy.

Conclusion

Each of these cult groups provides not only the life-meaning elements for the individual, but has in common the cardinal points made in chapter 2 and usually associated with cult groups in all ages; that is, they reject contemporary society and represent an attempt to set up a perfect order.

These two examples of cult practice, Communism and Mormon Fundamentalism, are thus shown to provide the same needs as do other cult systems, in spite of the fact that the actual causes to which these various groups are dedicated are in opposition to each other. People do embrace these persuasions with "fondness and devotion" and maintain them with "resolution and eagerness," not necessarily because they are based upon truth or the best good, but simply because they supply, at least for a time, these basic needs of cause, brotherhood, and rank.

Chapter Four

Premise and Logic

Introduction

The majority of people are carried along in the tradition they inherit and seldom take time to investigate the fundamentals upon which their daily actions are founded. However, it must be admitted that every persuasion has its share of intellectuals. Most religious and political movements have a rational basis. That is, the intellectuals have woven a logic structure that justifies the means used to arrive at the desired end.

If the casual student finds a system of thought to be illogical to him, it is only because he has failed to obtain the insider's perspective. Unless we have justification for assuming that our intellectual powers are greater than those of such men as St. Augustine, Karl Marx, or Martin Luther, we must admit that the systems they built seem to be internally consistent and logical.

If we wish to hold a debate, or attempt to challenge a champion of an opposing system by logic and argument, we will only learn that our efforts have failed to impress our opponent. Arguments that appear to be so profound to one party are meaningless to another because they are based upon a different *premise* (foundation or grounds).

It is not the logic structure that is open to question, but the premise or, as John Locke calls it, the "grounds" upon which it is built. A concrete and steel structure is supported by a foundation. As long as the foundation is secure, the structure will withstand the elements; but it is only necessary to undermine the foundation and the whole structure will collapse. Thus, it is not the system that is subject to question, but the premise upon which it is based, and if one accepts a premise as being true, one must accept the system in its entirety.

There are two characteristics of the premise that deserve attention. First, the premise upon which a system is built may be so simple and yet at the same time so subtle that many persons dedicated to a particular cause, have no conception whatsoever of that foundation upon which their actions are based. Second, the reason for the existence of so many opposing systems is that the premise upon which surviving systems are founded is itself often difficult, if not impossible, to prove or test.

That a premise cannot be proven or tested immediately is the reason opposing systems exist and survive side by side. If circumstances change and the premise becomes vulnerable and, in fact, disproven, the associated system, like the allegorical cement and steel building, will collapse and in time disappear. Given in this chapter is one example, the Pythagorian School, in which the premise was disproven, resulting in the end of that system. The premises are examined also for The Church of Jesus Christ of Latter-day Saints and the Fundamentalist cult groups, each of these premises being investigated in detail in the following chapters.

The Pythagorians

The Pythagorian School in Ancient Greece (540 B.C.) is an example of a system that was based upon a false premise. Once it was proven to be false, the Pythagorian School disappeared from the earth.

The Pythagorians were numerologists.[1] Today we use numbers as symbols to represent something. For example, the number 10 has no special meaning unless it is used to represent

[1]F. W. Kokomoor, *Mathematics in Human Affairs* (New York: Prentice Hall, Inc., 1942), pp. 15-16.

the quantity or number of something such as some object or event. The Pythagorians developed the remarkable philosophy that all things were number; that a number, rather than being a symbol, was the very essence of everything that existed—the principle of all being.

The numerical basis of this philosophy was reached through the observation of the importance of the form and size of objects, and relations existing between them. Any object, to be understood, must be weighed, measured, and given order among other objects. Without number, there could be neither law nor order. Thus, the Pythagorians came to the following conclusions: the number 1 was considered the essence of all things; 4 was the most perfect; 5 was the cause of color; 6, the cause of cold; 7, the cause of mind, health, and light; and 8, the octave, represented harmony, friendship, and love.

All geometrical figures were represented by numbers: A point was represented by 1, two points determined a straight line which was represented by the number 2, three noncollinear points determined a plane figure, and the number 4 stood for a geometrical solid.

The Pythagorian School had great influence on the social aspect of life, and attempted to develop moral strength, self-control, and induce action for good. They wanted to make their school a practical one in training for citizenship based upon a very deep and complex numerology. The Pythagorians submitted to a very severe discipline which flourished in many cities.

Of particular importance in the Pythagorian philosophy was the claim which they made that all numbers were rational; that is, could be written as a quotient of two integer numbers. However, it was proven that all numbers are not rational. In fact, the square root of 2 is an irrational number. This disconcerting fact was discovered by one of the Pythagorians,[2] who suppressed this knowledge, considering it to be an isolated case. However, the discovery of the irrational nature of the square root of 2 checked the advance of the school.

---

[2]Arnold Reymond, *History of the Sciences in Greco-Roman Antiquity,* trans. by Ruth Gheury Debray (New York: E. P. Dutton, 1927), 245 pages.

The Church of Jesus Christ of Latter-day Saints

The Church of Jesus Christ of Latter-day Saints is the church of the restoration, and claims that, by direct revelation, God and angels appeared to man to confer the priesthood and associated keys and to direct the re-establishment of the true Church. The Church further claims that the work of the kingdom is maintained only by continuous revelation from heaven. The Church declares its president to be the only man on earth in whom all the keys of the kingdom of God reside in their fulness; thus he is sustained as a prophet, seer, and revelator, and his inspired words are considered scripture.[3]

The Church members maintain that without the gift of direct revelation from heaven such as is received only by prophets, they are no better off than nonmembers. The scriptures are of great value and are considered sacred, but they are the history of God's revelations to other men at other times. Without new revelation, persons cannot know of their own callings. The great principle by which the true people of God are known and distinguished from all other people in all times is the principle of revelation through *living prophets.*

Thus, the premise upon which the Church of Jesus Christ is founded may be stated: *The true people of God in all ages are founded upon that kind of revelation that comes only through the living prophets of God.* The priesthood powers by which the principles and ordinances of salvation and exaltation are administered for the benefit of this world exist on the earth only when there are living prophets among the people. At all other times, the people are destitute and without the true knowledge of God or his plan for the welfare of mankind.

There exists a great deal of evidence to substantiate the premise of the Church. It applies to all ages and is not dependent upon the advent of the Christ, the scriptures, or of any special provision. It is in fact the basis of all that is sacred in scripture, history, and law.

---

[3]D&C 68:4.

Fundamentalism

There are many Fundamentalist groups that make differing claims. Only two of these claims will be considered here as being representative of the Fundamentalist movement in general. It will be seen that these claims have in common several important characteristics.

The Church of the Firstborn of the Fulness of Times is unique among the Fundamentalist cult groups in that it is the only one to legally incorporate a church organization. The Articles of Incorporation, signed by Joel F. LeBaron, were recorded September 21, 1955, by the Utah Secretary of State.[4] However, the leaders of the Church of the Firstborn of the Fulness of Times acknowledge all the prophets of The Church of Jesus Christ of Latter-day Saints, and accept the four standard works of the Church in their present form.

Many other cult groups exist that claim to be members of no organization except The Church of Jesus Christ of Latter-day Saints, and are distinguished only by their particular file leader. Like the Church of the Firstborn of the Fulness of Times, these groups accept The Church of Jesus Christ of Latter-day Saints as God's church, its president as a prophet of God, and the four standard works of the Church as scripture.

In each case, the Fundamentalists take exception to the teaching and practice of The Church of Jesus Christ of Latter-day Saints regarding the principle of plural marriage, united order, and other doctrines. These groups justify their actions in teaching and practicing concepts that go against the Church position, even though they acknowledge the Church as God's church, because of certain priesthood provisions that were alleged to have taken place under certain special conditions. It is this type of claim (namely, a special priesthood provision) that all Fundamentalist cult groups have in common, although the details of the various claims differ from one group to another.

---

[4]H. W. Richards, *A Reply to "The Church of the Firstborn of the Fulness of Times"* (Salt Lake City: Deseret Book Company, 1965), p. 2.

The Church of the Firstborn of the Fulness of Times

The church organized by Joel F. LeBaron and his associates maintains that there are two offices of the priesthood higher in authority than the First Presidency of The Church of Jesus Christ of Latter-day Saints. These two offices are President of the High (Melchizedek) Priesthood and the office of presiding patriarch.[5]

The LeBarons claim that Joseph Smith received the office of President of the High Priesthood from John the Beloved in the Kirtland Temple, April 3, 1836, and that he secretly ordained his friend, Benjamin F. Johnson, to this office some time before he entered Carthage Jail. This office was "hid with Christ in God"[6] until shortly before Benjamin F. Johnson died, when he ordained his grandson, Alma Dayer LeBaron, on about 11 November 1905. The LeBarons further claim that Alma Dayer LeBaron ordained his son, Joel F. LeBaron, on about 1 February 1951. At the time of this alleged ordination, Alma Dayer LeBaron had been excommunicated from the Church because of immorality associated with so-called plural marriage. The LeBaron group claims that Joel F. LeBaron is the last prophet to come and that he will still be living in the flesh when the coming of Christ takes place.[7]

According to the LeBarons, the second highest office in the priesthood is called the Priesthood of Aaron, the Second Priesthood, or the Patriarchal Priesthood, and this office is higher than the office of President of the Church but subordinate to the President of the High Priesthood.

The cultists claim that the Patriarchal Priesthood was restored by John the Baptist on May 15, 1829, to Joseph Smith and Oliver Cowdery. Since Joseph Smith was the first elder of the Church, in their reasoning he was the first patriarch to the Church. They claim that on April 3, 1836, when Joseph received the office of President of the High Priesthood, Oliver

---

[5]Ervil M. LeBaron, *Priesthood Expounded* (Mexico: Mexican Mission of the Church of the Firstborn of the Fulness of Times, August 1956), pp. 51-55.
[6]Ibid., p. 54.
[7]Richards, *A Reply*, p. 76.

became the presiding patriarch. Later this office was put upon Joseph Smith, Sr., who became the third patriarch to the Church. Still later, it was given to Hyrum Smith; then to Uncle John Smith in Carthage Jail the night before Joseph and Hyrum were martyred, for him to hold in trust.[8] They further claim that in due time the patriarchal office was put upon John Smith, the son of Hyrum. This office then passed from John Smith to John W. Woolley and to Joseph W. Musser (who died on March 29, 1954).

It is through these claims to priesthood authority that the Fundamentalist Church of the Firstborn of the Fulness of Times is carried out on an independent basis where the principle of plural marriage and other doctrines are practiced.

Other Fundamentalist Groups

Other of the independent Fundamentalist cult groups, with the exception of the Church of the Firstborn of the Fulness of Times, have been loosely organized under a visible voice, The Truth Publishing Company, Salt Lake City, Utah. The Truth publications present a concept of priesthood very similar to that of the Church of the Firstborn of the Fulness of Times but differing in some details. "There are three grand orders of Priesthood," the highest of these is President of the High (Melchizedek) Priesthood; the second is patriarch, which "is at the head of the Church . . . he presides over the President of the Church;" and the third is the Levitical Priesthood.[9]

The Fundamentalists claim there are two orders of apostles, the highest designated "High Priest Apostles," who must be personally ordained to the calling by Jesus himself. "His regularly constituted and authorized prophets *must* be ordained by *Him*."[10] This order of high priest apostle constitutes a quorum of seven men. "The Priesthood proper is presided over by a quorum of seven men holding the higher order of

---

[8]LeBaron, *Priesthood Expounded*, p. 17.

[9]Anonymous, *A Priesthood Issue*, (Salt Lake City: Truth Publishing Co., 1948), p. 7. Hereafter referred to as *A Priesthood Issue*.

[10]Ibid., p. 9, 10.

Priesthood."[11] "From this it is clearly seen that there is an apostolic order designated as 'The Apostleship of the Twelve,' which must be subordinate to the 'High Priest' Apostles . . . the members of which are designated as 'Friends'."[12]

The Fundamentalists claim that this higher priesthood can function outside of and independent of the Church, and that the Church is auxiliary to the high priesthood. Many years before the LeBaron movement began, the Fundamentalists referred to "the Church of the Firstborn whose membership comprise only those who obey the Lord in all things" and contrasted this with the "earthly institution called The Church of Jesus Christ of Latter-day Saints to which all classes of men become members."[13]

The Fundamentalists concede that the President of the Church was also President of the High Priesthood, and that the Twelve Apostles were of the higher order down until the time of President Wilford Woodruff. However, on September 27, 1886,

> John Taylor, not as President of the Church, but as President of the priesthood . . . under the direction of Joseph Smith who was present in the room in person, chose five men and set them apart to continue such [plural] marriages, after the Church should have discontinued them within its jurisdiction . . . . These five men were John W. Woolley, Lorin C. Woolley, George Q. Cannon, Charles H. Wilken, and Samuel Bateman. President Taylor's Second Counselor, Joseph F. Smith . . . was at the time in Hawaii performing a mission. He was sent for and received a like commission from John Taylor. . . . These six, then, with Wilford Woodruff . . . formed the Priesthood Presidency at that time.
>
> After the death of John Taylor, Wilford Woodruff, being the senior in ordination in the higher order of priesthood . . . issued a Manifesto stopping plural marriage within the Church — *doing so as President of the Church* — yet, in his priesthood capacity, he appointed men and set them apart . . . to perform such marriages, an act clearly within the functions of Priesthood and above the jurisdiction of the Church.[14]

---

[11]Ibid., p. 12.
[12]Ibid., p. 10.
[13]Ibid., p. 22.
[14]Ibid., p. 25.

This alleged ordination by President Taylor and the martyred Prophet, Joseph Smith, was performed in secret and continued in reserve until the Church began to ostracize those who practiced the principle of plural marriage. This secret provision is justified by the Fundamentalists on the alleged grounds that the principle of common consent applies only to the Church and not to the priesthood.

A statement by Lorin C. Woolley[15] dated September 22, 1929, describes this ordination by John Taylor and Joseph Smith:

> During the eight hours we were together, and while President Taylor was talking to us he frequently arose and stood above the floor, and his countenance and being were so enveloped by light and glory that it was difficult for us to look upon him. . . . He then set us apart and placed us under covenant that while we lived we would see to it that no year passed by without children being born in the principle of plural marriage. We were given authority to ordain others if necessary to carry this work on, they in turn to be given authority to ordain others when necessary under the direction of the worthy senior (by ordination), so that there should be no cessation in the work. . . . He said that in the time of the seventh President of this Church, the Church would go into *bondage both temporally and spiritually* and in that day the one Mighty and Strong spoken of in the 85th section of the Doctrine and Covenants would come.

He also said, "Some of you will be handled and ostracized and cast out from the Church by your brethren because of your faithfulness and integrity to this principle.[16]

Thus the Fundamentalists in general claim special priesthood provisions that were brought about in secret and were hidden up in reserve until a later time. It is not our objective at this point to investigate the truthfulness of these claims. The significant point to be made here is that the claims to authority rest upon alleged priesthood provisions given *secretly* to certain men, all but one of whom were long since dead before these claims were made known.

---

[15]Musser, *Hidden Revelations,* p. 30, 31.
[16]Ibid., pp. 29-31.

The law of Moses required that a person should not be put to death "at the mouth of one witness" but "at the mouth of two witnesses, or three witnesses, shall he that is worthy of death be put to death." The Lord recognized this *law of witnesses* when he said, "If I bear witness of myself, my witness is not true." Finally, the Lord declared, as recorded in the Doctrine and Covenants, "And in the mouth of two or three witnesses shall every word be established."[17]

The Prophet Joseph Smith received the Aaronic Priesthood from the resurrected John the Baptist, the Melchizedek Priesthood from Peter, James, and John, the keys from Moses, Elias and Elijah for each of their respective dispensations. If Joseph Smith had been alone, no one would have been under any obligation to accept his unsupported witness even though he recorded it; however, in each of these incidents Oliver Cowdery was present and was a recipient with the Prophet of these blessings.[18] Although no one was present with Joseph when the Father and the Son appeared to him in the First Vision, Sidney Rigdon was with him on another occasion when the Father and the Son appeared to them and together they testified:

> And now, after the many testimonies which have been given of him, this is the testimony, last of all, which we give of him: That he lives! For we saw him, even on the right hand of God; and we heard the voice bearing record that he is the Only Begotten of the Father.[19]

Thus, this vision to Joseph Smith and Sidney Rigdon brings the manifestation of the Father and the Son in this dispensation into accord with the law of witnesses.

There is no evidence that the alleged ordination of Benjamin F. Johnson ever occurred; in fact, the LeBarons claim that "it was hid with Christ in God."[20]

---

[17]Deuteronomy 17:6; John 5:31; D&C 6:28.

[18]D&C 13; 27:12; 110:11-16.

[19]Ibid., 76:22-23.

[20]A similar claim is made by other groups tracing their authority to Lorin C. Woolley, who was allegedly given the keys of the priesthood "to hold in trust as a deed in escrow." (Pierce, *3½ Years,* p. 77.)

Only one eyewitness testimony is claimed for the alleged ordination by John Taylor of certain men in 1886. This testimony given by Lorin C. Woolley forty-three years after the event, coming as it did upon the heels of a Church-sponsored purge of the Fundamentalists, does not fulfill the requirement given by the Lord that every word be established in the mouth of *two* or *three* witnesses. Woolley admitted in his account that "many of the things I forgot, but they are coming to me gradually." Furthermore, he had been excommunicated from the Church for practicing so-called plural marriage.[21]

Thus the premise upon which all Fundamentalist cult groups are founded may be stated as follows: *The Fundamentalists are founded upon alleged special priesthood provisions given in secret to men who are now dead and who left no testimonies of these events as required by the law of witnesses.*

Conclusion

Like any rational system, some of the logic of Fundamentalist theology is sound and self-consistent, as anyone who really understands it will agree. The major aspect of the Fundamentalist theology open to question is the premise upon which it is based. Like many opposing systems that exist in contemporary society, the premise upon which the Fundamentalists are based has been very carefully contrived so that no testimonies, no witnesses, no recorded history exists that can be examined to verify the alleged events.

The premise upon which the Fundamentalists are founded, "alleged special priesthood provisions given in secret to men who are now dead and who left no testimony of these events as required by the law of witnesses," is an example of "something in the nature of a general principle. The rejection of living prophets and the veneration of dead ones is not a folly limited to one nation or to one generation. It meets us throughout the long history of Israel as a sort of standard procedure."[22]

---

[21]Musser, *Hidden Revelations,* pp. 29, 30.

[22]Hugh Nibley, *The World and the Prophets* (Salt Lake City: Deseret Book Company, 1962), p. 6.

Orson Pratt stated that the person who rejects new revelation "rejects one of the great fundamental principles by which the people of God in all ages are clearly distinguished from every other people."[23]

By contrast, the premise upon which The Church of Jesus Christ of Latter-day Saints is founded is that "the kind of revelation that comes only through living prophets of God" is unique in that a great deal of evidence is available to demonstrate its truthfulness. In fact, as stated before, all that is sacred in scripture, history, and law was given through those thus founded. Persons who have been attracted by the seemingly rational basis of Fundamentalist teachings and who have become involved in cult practices should look deeper and examine the stability of the foundation upon which their teachings are based.

---

[23]Orson Pratt, *Orson Pratt's Works* (Salt Lake City: Deseret News Press, 1945), p. 68.

Chapter Five

The Priesthood and the Church

Introduction

The Fundamentalists define a new relationship between the priesthood and the Church to make their claims of special secret priesthood provisions more palatable. The relationship between Church, priesthood and kingdom is considered in this chapter.

The Fundamentalists claim that the priesthood can function outside and independent of the Church, and that the Church is auxiliary to the priesthood: "The Priesthood presides over the Church and in no way is subject to Church dictation"[1] and "since it was the Priesthood that organized the Church, and the Church is subordinate to the Priesthood, certainly the Church does not now, nor can it ever control the Priesthood."[2] As proof of this, the Fundamentalists cite the historical fact that Joseph Smith "introduced the practice of plural marriage among a few of his brethren without Church knowledge or consent."[3] "It being a Priesthood law, it did not concern the Church until Brigham Young introduced it to the Church in a special conference in the year 1852, when the Church received it by vote."[4] As additional proof, the Funda-

---

[1]Joseph W. Musser, *The Law of Plural Marriage* (Salt Lake City: The Truth Publishing Co., No date), p. 6.

[2]*A Priesthood Issue,* p. 22.

[3]Ibid., p. 24.

[4]Musser, *Plural Marriage,* p. 5.

mentalists cite the Council of Fifty, or Political Kingdom of God, as an organization acting under priesthood jurisdiction, established by Joseph Smith, which was declared to be separate from the Church.[5]

Using these citations, the Fundamentalists attempt to justify their actions as being under priesthood jurisdiction but independent of the Church. The Fundamentalists argue that they are doing no differently than Joseph Smith and his intimate followers did when they practiced plural marriage for some twenty years "wholly aside from and independent of the Church,"[6] until it was made a Church rule in 1852.

The Church

The question introduced by the Fundamentalists when they discuss the relationship between the Church, the kingdom, and the priesthood revolves around the definition of the word *Church* and the relationship between priesthood, office and keys.

Any man who holds the Melchizedek Priesthood has as much priesthood power as does any prophet who ever lived, and no man can possess that priesthood except "he that is called of God as was Aaron."[7]

Since the priesthood is greater than any *office* in the priesthood, no office adds any power, dignity, or authority to the priesthood. All offices derive their rights, virtues, prerogatives, and powers from the priesthood. "All other authorities or offices in the church are appendages to this [Melchizedek] priesthood."[8] These offices grow out of the priesthood and are therefore less than or supplemental to the priesthood.

Now consider the offices of deacon, teacher, priest, elder, seventy, high priest, bishop, patriarch, and apostle. Are they offices of the Church or offices of the priesthood? We often think of the Church as a legal corporate body; it is so, but only

---

[5]*A Priesthood Issue,* p. 16.
[6]Ibid., p. 21.
[7]Hebrews 5:4.
[8]D&C 107:5.

to fulfill certain legal requirements of the law of the land. In the year 1887, the Edmunds-Tucker Act became law. This act disincorporated the Church and escheated its property. However, the offices listed above continued to exist during this time. When the Church was reinstated as a corporate entity, it was not necessary to reordain everyone, because these offices do not depend upon an act of incorporation.

Orson Pratt defines a kingdom in general as a government containing a king, his authorized representatives, and subjects. As for the kingdom of God, Christ is the king, his authorized representatives are those who hold the priesthood, and the kingdom is governed by those of the priesthood who are appointed to the various offices required by the king to conduct the affairs of the kingdom. Subjects of the kingdom become so by submitting to the entrance requirements set up by the king and administered by his authorized servants.[9]

We read in both the Bible[10] and the Doctrine and Covenants[11] that the keys of the kingdom are given to the apostles who are first in the church.[12] Parley P. Pratt, one of the original Twelve Apostles stated: "The fact is, when the order of the kingdom is fully established, the Twelve are the only general officers of the church whose jurisdiction is *universal*."[13] (Even the First Presidency receives its powers ultimately from the Twelve who are the repository of the priesthood keys on earth.) The word *universal* is all-inclusive and as used here precludes any priesthood action independent of the Twelve and the Church *except* when the kingdom is not fully established.

Thus, in this context it is clearly impossible to differentiate between the offices of the priesthood, the Church, and the kingdom of God—they are one and the same. These terms—*Church* and *kingdom*—are used synonymously and are both composed of the offices and appendages of the Melchizedek

---

[9]*Orson Pratt's Works*, pp. 31-45.

[10]Matthew 16:19.

[11]D&C 81:2, 112:16, 124:128, 143.

[12]1 Corinthians 12:28.

[13]*Millennial Star*, (A periodical first published at Manchester, England, May, 1840), 5 (1845):152.

Priesthood. The Fundamentalist postulate that "the Church is not a Priesthood organization, but is directed by the Priesthood"[14] is inconsistent with this statement made by B. H. Roberts: "The church . . . may be said *to be* the collected authority of *all* the quorums of the priesthood combined—the aggregation of God's authority in the earth, in relation to things religious. Such is the church."[15]

The Priesthood Keys and Offices

The priesthood is a latent power, meaning that, unless he has the keys, the recipient cannot use the priesthood he holds. Keys are the right of presidency, the power to control and regulate. In symbolic language, the keys open the door to the use of the priesthood. The keys of the sealing power, for example, open the door to use of the sealing power. In other words, the keys of the priesthood, or the keys of sealing power, are the power and right by which priesthood and sealings are governed, controlled, and regulated.

Thus, the keys and power of the kingdom are the right and power to preside over and direct all the affairs of the kingdom of God on earth.[16] This kingdom, at the present time, consists of "all the collected authority of all the quorums of the priesthood combined" or, in other words, the Church.

When the gospel was restored, the Lord revealed knowledge, priesthood and keys, but not all at once. From time to time the Lord gave Joseph and his associates various parts of these powers until they had all been conferred upon men.

These keys were restored by

> the voice of Michael, the archangel; the voice of Gabriel, and of Raphael, and of divers angels, from Michael or Adam down to the present time, all declaring their dispensation, their rights, their keys, their honors, their majesty and glory, and the power of their priesthood; giving line upon line, precept upon precept, here a little, and

[14]*A Priesthood Issue,* footnote p. 4.

[15]B. H. Roberts, *Outlines of Ecclesiastical History,* 3rd ed. (Salt Lake City: Deseret News Co., 1902), p. 342. Also quoted in *A Priesthood Issue,* p. 16. (Italics added.)

[16]Bruce R. McConkie, "Cultism as Practiced by the So-Called Church of the Firstborn of the Fulness of Times" (Unpublished-mimeographed), p. 17.

there a little; giving us consolation by holding forth that which is to come, confirming our hope.[17]

Even though the Prophet Joseph Smith received the Melchizedek Priesthood and had been ordained an apostle by Peter, James, and John,[18] he did not at that time possess all the keys necessary to build up the kingdom. After he received the keys associated with the endowment, Joseph withheld them from the Saints until the Nauvoo Temple could be completed. However, just before the martyrdom of the Prophet, he called the Twelve together and bestowed upon them *all* the keys of the kingdom. In a proclamation to the Church in the Eastern States, Parley P. Pratt, one of the Twelve, describes this event.

> Again the people have not chosen the twelve apostles of this last dispensation; but God has chosen them, and conferred on them the apostleship; and this by revelation, through his servant Joseph, even as Moses called and made Aaron a priest, or as Jesus called and ordained the other Twelve. . . .
>
> We [the Twelve] hold the keys of the ministry and ordinances of salvation in this last kingdom: and if the people choose to be benefitted by them, it is their own blessing; if not, it is their own neglect. They cannot essentially add or diminish anything to our authority, or to our eternal power and glory. Our God can work and enable us to work, either with or without their means or their aid. And, in either case, the result of our labours will be the restoration of the kingdom and government of God.
>
> Hear it then, ye people; this is the destiny of the small, the despised church and kingdom of God, as established by him through the instrumentality of our murdered — martyred prophet. For this he lived and laboured; and for this he died.
>
> This great and good man was led, before his death, to call the Twelve together, from time to time, and to instruct them in all things pertaining to the kingdom, ordinances, and government of God. He often observed that he was laying the foundation, but it would remain for the Twelve to complete the building. Said he, "I know not why; but for some reason I am constrained to hasten my preparation, and to confer upon the Twelve all the ordinances, keys, covenants, endowments, and sealing ordinances of the priesthood, and so set before them a pattern in all things pertaining to the sanctuary and the endowment therein."

---

[17]D&C 128:21.
[18]Ibid., 27:12.

Having done this, he rejoiced exceedingly; for, said he, the Lord is about to lay the burden on your shoulders and let me rest awhile; and if they kill me, continued he, the kingdom of God will roll on, as I have now finished the work which was laid upon me, by committing to you all things for the building up of the kingdom according to the heavenly vision, and the pattern shown me from heaven. With many conversations like this, he comforted the minds of the Twelve, and prepared them for what was soon to follow.

He proceeded to confer on Elder Young, the President of the Twelve, the keys of the sealing power, as conferred in the last days by the spirit and power of Elijah, in order to seal the hearts of the fathers to the children, and the hearts of the children to the fathers, lest the whole earth should be smitten with a curse.

This last key of the priesthood is the most sacred of all, and *pertains exclusively to the first presidency of the church,* without whose sanction and approval or authority, no sealing blessing shall be administered pertaining to things of the resurrection and the life to come.

After giving them a very short charge to do all things according to the pattern, he quietly surrendered his liberty and his life into the hands of his bloodthirsty enemies, and all this to save the people for whom he had so long laboured from threatened vengeance.

Thus nobly fell our worthy founder and leader in the very bloom of life; and thus the responsibility of bearing off the kingdom triumphantly now rests upon the Twelve.

He has organized the kingdom of God. — We will extend its domain.

He has restored the fulness of the Gospel. — We will spread it abroad.

He has laid the foundation of Nauvoo. — We will build it up.

He has laid the foundation of the Temple. — We will bring up the top-stone with shouting.

He has kindled a fire. — We will fan the flame.

He has kindled up the dawn of a day of glory. — We will bring it to its meridian splendour.

He was a "little one," and became a thousand. — We are a small one, and will become a strong nation.

In short, he quarried the stone from the mountain; we will cause it to become a great mountain and fill the whole earth.[19]

---

[19]*Millennial Star* 5 (1845):149-153. (Italics added.) Reference to this event was made by Orson Hyde: "Before I went east on the 4th of April last, we were in council with Brother Joseph almost every day for weeks, says Brother Joseph in

The procedure is the same today. A man must have the priesthood conferred upon him; afterwards he is set apart or ordained to an office and is given all the keys pertaining to that office and calling. Each time a new apostle is ordained and set apart to serve as a member of the Council of the Twelve, he is given all the keys of the kingdom, but their full operation remains dormant in him unless he becomes the senior or presiding apostle. The Lord said, "I have appointed unto my servant Joseph to hold this power in the last days, and there is never but one on the earth at a time on whom this power and the keys of this priesthood are conferred."[20] And the Lord promised Joseph, "The keys of this kingdom shall never be taken from you, while thou art in the world, neither in the world to come; nevertheless, through you shall the oracles be given to another, yea, even unto the *church*."[21]

Plural Marriage Before 1852

Plural marriage was not a *general* principle of the Church until it had been presented by the First Presidency in a *general* conference and accepted by the Church in sustaining vote. However, the significant fact is that the practice of plural marriage by *limited* members of the Church before 1852 and by the Church in *general* after 1852 was under the control of the First Presidency of the Church, "without whose sanction and

---

one of those councils there is something going to happen; I don't know what it is, but the Lord bids me to hasten and give you your endowment before the temple is finished. He conducted us through every ordinance of the holy priesthood, and when he had gone through with all the ordinances he rejoiced very much, and says, now if they kill me you have got all the keys, and all the ordinances and you can confer them upon others, and the hosts of Satan will not be able to tear down the kingdom, as fast as you will be able to build it up; and now says he on your shoulders will rest the responsibility of leading this people, for the Lord is going to let me rest a while." *Millennial Star,* 5 (1844):104. Wilford Woodruff testified of this event, that "when they received their endowment, and actually received the keys of the kingdom of God, and oracles of God, keys of revelation, and the pattern of heavenly things; and thus addressing the Twelve, exclaimed, 'upon your shoulders the kingdom rests, and you must round up your shoulders and bear it, for I have had to do it until now. But now the responsibility rests upon you. It mattereth not what becomes of me.' " *Millennial Star,* 5 (1844):109.

[20]D&C 132:7.

[21]Ibid., 90:3-4. (Italics added.)

approval or authority, no sealing blessings shall be administered,"[22] to use the words of Parley P. Pratt again.

The Prophet Joseph Smith first learned of the law of plural marriage by revelation in 1831 or 1832, and he later confided this information to his close and trusted associates. These men were all of New England puritan stock; the idea of plural marriage went against their sensibilities; and they delayed putting the principle into practice. According to Eliza R. Snow, Joseph hesitated "until an angel of God stood by him with drawn sword, and told him that, unless he moved forward and established plural marriage, his priesthood would be taken from him and he should be destroyed."[23]

Brigham Young confessed that when the Prophet first told him about the law of plural marriage, "it was the first time in my life that I desired the grave and I could hardly get over it for a long time."[24]

Joseph Smith and his associates began to practice plural marriage, in accordance with the angelic command, but hesitated to make a public announcement of either the doctrine or the practice of it. They realized that public knowledge of this doctrine would add to the severe persecutions that the Saints were subjected to, persecutions that eventually led to the Prophet's death. The doctrine of plural marriage was introduced into the Church in general only after the exodus from Nauvoo and after the Saints were secured in the Mountain West.

The introduction of the principle and practice of plural marriage into the Church in general was accomplished in the same way as any other part of the gospel; it was always controlled and administered by the First Presidency who, with the Twelve, hold the keys of the kingdom, and it was presented to the Church conference subsequent to the revelation. The

---

[22]*Millennial Star,* 5(1845):151.

[23]Eliza R. Snow, *Biography of Lorenzo Snow* (Salt Lake City: Deseret News Co., 1884), p. 70.

[24]Quoted in William A. Linn, *The Story of the Mormons* (New York: MacMillan Co., 1923), p. 280.

only unusual aspect concerning the principle of plural marriage was the long delay between the revelation and the sustaining vote of the general conference.

The Council of Fifty or Political Kingdom of God

It is true that the Prophet Joseph organized a "Council of Fifty" that is also referred to as the "Political Kingdom of God." Brigham Young stated in 1855:

> As was observed by Brother Pratt that the kingdom is actually organized and the inhabitants of the earth do not know it. If this people know anything about it, all right; it is organized preparatory to taking effect in the due time of the Lord, and in the manner that shall please Him. As observed by one of the speakers this morning that kingdom *grows out of the Church of Jesus Christ of Latter-day Saints,* but it is not the church, for a man may be a legislator in that body which will issue laws to sustain the inhabitants of the earth in their individual rights and still not belong to The Church of Jesus Christ *at all.* And further, though a man may not even believe in any religion, it would be perfectly right, when necessary, to give him the privilege of holding a seat among that body which will make laws to govern all the nations of the earth and control those who make no profession of religion at all; for that body would be governed, controlled and dictated to acknowledge others in those rights which they wish to enjoy themselves. Then the Latter-day Saints would be protected, if a kingdom of this kind was on the earth, the same as all other people.[25]

Brigham Young, speaking of the political kingdom of God in the same sermon, stated:

> The Church of Jesus Christ will produce this government, and cause it to grow and spread, and it will be a shield round about the Church. And under the influence and power of the Kingdom of God, the Church of God will rest secure and dwell in safety, without taking the trouble of governing and controlling the whole earth. The Kingdom of God will do this, it will control the kingdoms of the world.[26]

---

[25]Joseph Smith, *History of The Church of Jesus Christ of Latter-day Saints,* 7 vols., B. H. Roberts, ed. (Salt Lake City: Deseret Book Co., 1956), 7:381-382. Hereafter referred to as Smith, *History of the Church.*

[26]*Journal of Discourses,* 2:316-317.

Orson Pratt, in a sermon of 1872, emphasized that the political kingdom of God grows out of the Church when he stated:

> There is now organized on the earth a Government which never will be broken as former Governments have been. This will stand for ever. It began very small — only six members were organized in this Government on Tuesday the 6th day of April, 1830.[27]

According to Daniel's dream, the kingdom of God was likened to a stone which, loosened from the mountain top without hands, would destroy all worldly governments and kingdoms and finally fill the whole earth.[28]

The creation of a political kingdom to prepare for the millennial reign of Christ was the major goal of the Council of Fifty. This idea is in keeping with the Mormon belief that God requires active participation of man to fulfill his purposes.

Brigham Young indicated that this political kingdom was an outgrowth of the Church, which means that it was created and operated under the First Presidency and the Twelve who hold "all the keys of the kingdom." This is in accordance with a declaration issued at the completion of the Salt Lake Temple in 1893, by a convocation of 115 select Church leaders, who unanimously affirmed that

> the presidency of the church are set to govern and control the affairs of the Church and Kingdom of God . . . that upon their shoulders rests the responsibility of teaching, governing, controlling and counseling the church and kingdom of God in *all* things on the earth.[29]

The political kingdom had to be separate from the Church, at least in the minds of the Church leaders, because of the strong commitment given to the principle of the separation of church and state by the Prophet.[30] It is likely that the early

---

[27]Ibid., 15:45.

[28]Daniel 2:44-45.

[29]Klaus J. Hansen, "The Metamorphosis of the Kingdom of God: Toward a Reinterpretation of Mormon History," *Dialogue* 1 (Autumn 1966):74. (Italics added.)

[30]D&C 101:76-80.

Church leaders were never able to work out, in a consistent way, the implications of this political-religious kingdom concept.

However, the Prophet expected that the millennial reign was very near, as was indicated by his prophecy on war beginning in South Carolina that would envelop the earth and lead to the "full end of all nations."[31] Patriarch Benjamin F. Johnson, an original member of the Council of Fifty, remarked, "We were over seventy years ago taught by our leaders to believe that the coming of Christ and the millennial reign was much nearer than we believe it to be now."[32]

Brigham Young claimed that "the Constitution and laws of the United States resembles a theocracy more closely than any government now on earth. . . . Even now the form of government of the United States differs but little from the Kingdom of God."[33]

The Church leaders, through the Council of Fifty, pushed the nomination of the Mormon Prophet to the presidency of the United States. Several members of the council were sent to negotiate a possible tract of land in Texas as a settling place for the Saints. An alternative location was investigated in the trans-Mississippi West. The Council of Fifty launched the state of Deseret.[34]

As the Mormon people moved ever closer to the mainstream of American life and the millennial expectations weakened, the Council of Fifty outlived its usefulness and Mormon nationalism associated with a political kingdom faded. However, the Council of Fifty completed its important mission of establishing a home for the Saints.[35]

---

[31]D&C 87.

[32]Letter of Benjamin F. Johnson to George S. Gibbs, April-October 1903, p. 18, (Brigham Young University Library). Quoted in Hansen, "Metamorphosis" *Dialogue* 1 (Autumn 1966):76.

[33]*Journal of Discourses,* 6:342, 345.

[34]Hansen, "Metamorphosis," *Dialogue* (Autumn 1966):63-68.

[35]Hyrum L. Andrus, *Joseph Smith and World Government* (Salt Lake City: Hawkes Publications, 1972), 122 pages. This little book gives an excellent treatise on the political kingdom: its relationship to the Church, its role in settling the Church in the West during the great exodus from Illinois, and its future millennial role.

Conclusion

The Fundamentalists are founded upon alleged special priesthood provisions given in secret, which permit them to claim authority going back to the Prophet Joseph Smith to act independently of the Church. They attempt to substantiate these claims by interpreting the early practice of plural marriage by the Prophet, without Church knowledge or consent, and the organization of the Council of Fifty, an organization independent of the Church, as examples of independent priesthood action.

We have seen in this chapter that all of these actions were under the direct control of the First Presidency and the Quorum of the Twelve, who possess all the keys of the kingdom pertaining to all the saving and exalting ordinances of the gospel, including sealings.

On occasion the Lord has called a prophet to act independent of any existing organization. This is exactly what happened when Joseph Smith acted in the capacity of prophet before the Church was organized. The key to understanding this is given by Parley P. Pratt, quoted above: "The fact is, when the order of the kingdom is *fully* established, the Twelve are the only general officers of the church whose jurisdiction is *universal.*" Instances of independent prophetic action occurred only when there was "no organized branch of the church," so that a sustaining vote could not be taken. But whenever the Church or kingdom is fully organized, as it has been since the original Twelve were given all the keys of the kingdom, the Twelve have *universal* jurisdiction. The use of the word *universal* precludes any priesthood action independent of the Twelve or the Church.

Chapter Six

Church Unity

Introduction

The previous chapter identified the Church, kingdom and priesthood as one and the same, all unified and directed through the First Presidency and Quorum of the Twelve. The Fundamentalists claim that the priesthood can act independent of the Church; however, in another context they must claim Church membership. This is because the scriptures explicitly state that salvation cannot be found outside of the Church. Thus, the Fundamentalists must claim to be independent of the Church and members of the Church simultaneously. The only way this can be accomplished is to redefine what is meant by the term *Church.* The subject of this chapter deals with this question of church identity, unity, and order.

Who Belongs to the Church?

The Lord declared, "And wo unto them who are cut off from my church, for the same are overcome of the world."[1] Also,

> whosoever belongeth to my church need not fear, for such shall inherit the kingdom of heaven. . . . Behold, this is my doctrine — whosoever repenteth and cometh unto me, the same is my church. Whosoever declareth more or less than this, the same is not for me, but is against me; therefore, he is not of my church. And now,

[1]D&C 50:8.

behold, whosoever is of my church, and endureth of my church to the end, him will I establish upon my rock, and the gates of hell shall not prevail against them.[2]

These explicit statements result in a use of the word *church* by the Fundamentalists that is not unlike the historical Protestant development of the concept of the "invisible church." The Protestants had to liberalize the concept of church to include themselves as well as the Catholic Church from which they owe their origins. Calvin maintained that "the true church only exists when the pure Word is preached and the sacraments are rightly administered."[3] Thus, the reformation rejected the Catholic basis of authority and made the word of God, or the biblical scripture, the sole source of authority, maintaining that the true church exists only where and when the "pure word" is the basis for efficacy. Based upon this premise, any sect—providing it preaches the Bible in its "purity"—is the true church of Jesus Christ. From this premise spring the multitude of Protestant sects in the world today. Such liberalizing of the concept of church resulted in complete abandonment of the principle of *unity,* one of the basic Christian tenets.

The Fundamentalists have used the phrase, *Church of the Firstborn,* found in the Doctrine and Covenants,[4] and declared it to be the church "whose membership comprise only those who obey the Lord in all things," and contrasted this with the "earthly institution called The Church of Jesus Christ of Latter-day Saints to which all classes of men become members."[5] This name, Church of the Firstborn, was in the Truth publications long before the LeBarons organized an incorporated body under that title. Further, other schisms within the Fundamentalist groups have resulted in a whole class of subgroups, each making different claims to authority. Thus, like protestantism, Fundamentalism has led to a complete abandonment of the principle of unity.

---

[2]Ibid., 10:55, 67-69.

[3]Wilhelm Niesel, *The Theology of Calvin,* trans. by Harold Knight (Philadelphia: Westminster Press, 1956), pp. 194-197.

[4]D&C 76:54; 67; 77:11; 78:21; 93:22; 107:19.

[5]*A Priesthood Issue,* p. 22.

The Lord has made it clear so that none need to be confused about how to identify his Church:

> Verily, thus saith the Lord . . . unto all the elders and people of *my Church of Jesus Christ of Latter-day Saints. . . .* For thus shall my church be called in the last days, even The Church of Jesus Christ of Latter-day Saints. Verily I say unto you all: Arise and shine forth, that thy light may be a standard for the nations; And that the gathering together upon the land of Zion, and upon her stakes, may be for a defense, and for a refuge from the storm, and from wrath when it shall be poured out without mixture upon the whole earth.[6]

In these statements the Lord has given a definition of his Church:

> Whosoever belongeth to *my church [of Jesus Christ of Latter-day Saints]* need not fear, for such shall inherit the kingdom of heaven.
>
> Wo unto them who are cut off from *my church [of Jesus Christ of Latter-day Saints]*, for the same are overcome of the world.[7]

Fundamentalists who have been excommunicated from the Church claim that it is no different than moving from one ward to another—that their names are removed from one record and added to the other. This is not so, since by their actions they fail to sustain the First Presidency and the Twelve. They reject the operation of the keys of the priesthood as exercised by their stake president and bishop.

The Law of Common Consent

The Fundamentalists acknowledge the law of common consent as applied to the Church, but claim that this law does not apply to the priesthood. They claim that

> John Taylor, not as President of the Church, but as President of the Priesthood, took certain action September 27, 1886. Had that action been taken as President of the Church, to render it legal, the Church would necessarily have had to approve it by vote, as it later did the Manifesto of Wilford Woodruff; as "all things must be

---

[6]D&C 115:1-6. (Italics added.)
[7]Ibid., 10:55; 50:8.

done by common consent of the Church." (Doctrine and Covenants 26:2). Acting, however, in purely a Priesthood capacity as President Taylor did, he was within his rights and the Church was not involved.[8]

This claim of the Fundamentalists that the law of common consent is a Church law and not a priesthood law, is necessary to justify the secrecy associated with the provision of 1886 upon which their present actions are founded.

This concept of secrecy associated with priesthood orders acting independently of the Church is meaningless, since it has been shown already that the Church is "the collected authority of all the quorums of the priesthood combined,"[9] that the keys of sealing pertain exclusively to the First Presidency of the Church, and that Christ's church is The Church of Jesus Christ of Latter-day Saints.

In addition, the concept of priesthood acting without the consent or knowledge of people who are dependent upon the ministration of those secret priesthood keys and powers for their salvation and exaltation, is in direct conflict with the concept of free agency. It is partly because of God's concern for man's free agency that he never has permitted nor will he ever permit priesthood to function without the consent or knowledge of the people.

Unity

One time Jesus cast out a devil from a man who was both blind and dumb, healing him. When the Pharisees heard it, they said:

> This fellow doth not cast out devils, but by Beelzebub the prince of the devils. And Jesus knew their thoughts, and said unto them, Every kingdom divided against itself . . . shall not stand: And if Satan cast out Satan, he is divided against himself; how shall then his kingdom stand?[10]

In his final prayer, Jesus prayed for unity among his disciples:

---

[8] *A Priesthood Issue,* p. 25.
[9] Roberts, *Ecclesiastical History,* p. 342.
[10] Matthew 12:24-26.

> Neither pray I for these alone, but for them also which shall believe on me through their word; that they all may be one; as thou, Father, art in me, and I in thee, that they also may be one in us: that the world may believe that thou hast sent me. And the glory which thou gavest me I have given them; that they may be one, even as we are one.[11]

Fundamentalists claim that God called certain men in the so-called "Provision of 1886" to continue the practice of plural marriage, and gave these men the keys of the priesthood necessary to perform those ordinances. Such commandments given in secret would lead inevitably to the formation of splinter groups. No one could have faith in a God who acted in such a capricious manner. Joseph Smith made this point clear in the *Lectures on Faith*, when he said:

> And again, the idea that he is a God of truth and cannot lie, is equally as necessary to the exercise of faith in him as the idea of his unchangeableness. For without the idea that he was a God of truth and could not lie, the confidence necessary to be placed in his word in order to the exercise of faith in him would not exist. But having the idea that he is not man, that he cannot lie, it gives power to the minds of men to exercise faith in him.[12]

The apostle Paul provided the same idea when he said, "For if the trumpet give an uncertain sound, who shall prepare himself to the battle?"[13]

Jesus said that we must be one "that the world may believe that thou hast sent me [Jesus]," and he also said, "And this gospel of the kingdom shall be preached in all the world for a witness unto all nations; and then shall the end come."[14] The world would not be encouraged to accept the gospel if we taught that God was responsible for secret provisions and conflict within the kingdom.

A similar condition arose in ancient Galatia, one of Paul's missionary fields. Some converts had been teaching the Galatians that it was necessary to obey the Jewish law of circum-

---

[11]John 17:20-22.

[12]Joseph Smith, "Lectures on Faith," 3:22, *Discourses on the Holy Ghost,* 4th ed. (Salt Lake City: Bookcraft, 1964), p. 122.

[13]1 Corinthians 14:8.

[14]Matthew 24:14.

cision. They were not preaching a false Christ or leading them away from the Church; they were just adding one teaching, one commandment of the Lord that he no longer required of his people. Note Paul's rebuke:

> I marvel that ye are so soon removed from him that called you into the grace of Christ unto another gospel: which is not another; but there be some that trouble you, and would pervert the gospel of Christ. But though we, or an angel from heaven, preach any other gospel unto you than that which we have preached unto you, let him be accursed.[15]

There is only one true doctrine and only one gospel. Two different groups cannot teach different doctrines and still be teaching the same gospel. Suppose an alleged revelation is given for the Church to someone not the president of the Church. "Let him be accursed," said Paul.

> And this shall be a law unto you, that ye receive not the teachings of any [except "him whom I have appointed unto you"] that shall come before you as revelations or commandments; and this I give unto you that you may not be deceived, that you may know they are not of me. For verily I say unto you, that he that is ordained of me shall come in at the gate and be ordained as I have told you before, to teach those revelations which you have received and shall receive through him whom I have appointed.[16]

This was the word of the Lord on this subject through the Prophet Joseph Smith. And, finally, the Lord said, "Be one; and if ye are not one ye are not mine."[17]

The apostle Paul, speaking of the role of the priesthood in the kingdom states:

> Now, therefore ye are no more strangers and foreigners, but fellowcitizens with the saints, and of the household of God; and are built upon the foundation of the apostles and prophets, Jesus Christ himself being the chief corner stone.[18]

Paul compares the kingdom with a body: "For as the body is one, and hath many members, and all the members of that

[15]Galatians 1:6-8.
[16]D&C 43:5-7.
[17]Ibid., 38:27.
[18]Ephesians 2:19-20.

one body, being many, are one body: so also is Christ." And further: "And God hath set some in the church, first apostles, secondarily prophets, thirdly teachers, after that miracles, then gifts of healings, helps, governments, diversities of tongues."[19] Paul has said that this priesthood organization with apostles at the helm is the church and body of Christ.

Paul explains why the Lord did establish the Church and kingdom on the foundation of apostles and prophets:

> And he gave some, apostles; and some, prophets; and some, evangelists; and some, pastors and teachers; for the perfecting of the saints, for the work of the ministry, for the edifying of the body of Christ: Till we all come in the unity of the faith, and of the knowledge of the Son of God, unto a perfect man, unto the measure of the stature of the fulness of Christ: That we henceforth be no more children, tossed to and fro, and carried about with every wind of doctrine, by the sleight of men, and cunning craftiness, whereby they lie in wait to deceive; but speaking the truth in love, may grow up into him in all things, which is the head, even Christ.[20]

Christ established us upon the apostles until we come to a unity of the faith and unto a perfection like Christ. This is necessary so we will not be tossed to and fro and carried about with every wind of doctrine.

The Lord also said, "Behold, mine house is a house of order, saith the Lord God, and not a house of confusion . . . . will I receive at your hands that which I have not appointed?"[21] When we receive a call from God we may know it is of his appointment and not be deceived, because it will come through the apostles and prophets; that is, the First Presidency and the Twelve. Furthermore, the Lord requires that: "No person is to be ordained to any office in this church, where there is a regularly organized branch of the same, without the vote of that church."[22] "For all things must be done in order and by common consent in the church, by the prayer of faith."[23]

---

[19]1 Corinthians 12:12, 28.
[20]Ephesians 4:11-15.
[21]D&C 132:8, 10.
[22]Ibid., 20:65.
[23]Ibid., 28:13.

Conclusion

The Lord has provided order and unity in the kingdom so we may know the truth and not be deceived. He has defined his Church as The Church of Jesus Christ of Latter-day Saints. He has established the law of common consent and built his Church upon the First Presidency and Quorum of the Twelve. The revealing of priesthood powers and keys has been in harmony with the divine law of witnesses. The so-called "Provision of 1886" would nullify all these laws and principles, making the gospel inconsistent so that obedience to one principle requires the Lord to abrogate other true principles. This is the essence of the "Provision of 1886" and other Fundamentalist claims to special priesthood provisions.

Chapter Seven

Priesthood Orders

Introduction

It has been shown in previous chapters that the Church consists of the "collected authority of all the quorums of the priesthood combined," that the power of the First Presidency and Quorum of the Twelve is universal, that sealing power pertains exclusively to the First Presidency, and that the practice of plural marriage and the political kingdom of God have been under the jurisdiction of the First Presidency. It therefore should not be necessary to consider the claims that Fundamentalists make to special priesthood orders.

However, since these claims are used by the Fundamentalists to substantiate their premise of secret priesthood provisions, some of these claims are considered in detail in this chapter.

The Fundamentalists postulate that there are special orders of priesthood of which the Church has no knowledge, orders that can act independent of the Church. These claims are used by the Fundamentalists to provide a theological basis for independent action and priesthood authority going back to the Prophet Joseph Smith.

The High Priesthood

The Fundamentalists teach that the President of the High Priesthood (Melchizedek) and the President of the Church are two distinct offices that are not necessarily held by the same man and that the office of President of the High Priesthood is higher or superior to the office of President of the Church. This notion that the President of the Church and the President of the High Priesthood are separate offices is contrary to revelation, for the Lord defined these as one and the same: "And again, the duty of the President of the office of the High Priesthood *is to preside* over the whole church, and to be like unto Moses."[1]

The President of the office of the High Priesthood is by definition President of the Church. The President of the High Priesthood would not be subject to councils of the Church in case of transgression if this were not so. "And inasmuch as a President of the High Priesthood shall transgress, he shall be had in remembrance before the common council of the church, who shall be assisted by twelve counselors of the High Priesthood."[2]

Wilford Woodruff was sustained as President of the Church at the April conference of 1889. He said:

> This seventh day of April, 1889, is one of the most important days of my life, for I was made President of The Church of Jesus Christ of Latter-day Saints by the unanimous vote of ten thousand of them. The vote was first taken by quorums and then by the entire congregation as in the case of President John Taylor. *This is the highest office ever conferred upon any man in the flesh.* It came to me in the eighty-third year of my life.[3]

The Apostleship and Keys of the Kingdom

The Fundamentalists teach that there are two orders of apostles; namely, high priest apostles who are over or superior to the Twelve, and the Quorum of the Twelve. Their literature states that "the priesthood proper is presided over by a quorum of seven men holding the higher order of priesthood,"[4] and that they act "under direction of a worthy senior . . . so that there should be no cessation in the work [performing of so-

---

[1]D&C 107:91. (Italics added.)

[2]Ibid., 107:82.

[3]Mathias F. Cowley, ed., *Wilford Woodruff* (Salt Lake City: Deseret News Press, 1909), p. 564. (Italics added.)

[4]*A Priesthood Issue,* p. 12.

called plural marriages],"[5] and that this council has acted independently of the Church since the time of Wilford Woodruff.[6]

The evidence given for this claim is the fact that the original Twelve were called and ordained to that office and that about nine years later, just before the Prophet's martyrdom, the Prophet bestowed upon them additional keys of authority. This proves, they say, that there are different orders of apostles having different keys.

Furthermore, they say that "to become a qualified apostle of Jesus Christ as before stated, one must know Him personally . . . receive their personal anointings from the Master himself" and, as "His regular constituted and authorized prophets, *must* be ordained by *Him*."[7] As proof of this they cite from the *Teachings of the Prophet Joseph Smith*:

> All Priesthood is Melchizedek, but there are different portions or degrees of it. That portion which brought Moses to speak with God face to face was taken away; but that which brought the ministry of angels remained. All the prophets had the Melchizedek Priesthood and were ordained by God Himself.[8]

Thus, by implication, the so-called high priest apostles have had the Savior minister personally to and ordain each of them.

In the absence of complete records we cannot know precisely how each of the ancient prophets received the priesthood. However, priesthood ordination of mortals is a function of tangible beings and not of spirit beings. This would rule out Jesus Christ (the pre-mortal Jehovah) prior to his receiving an earthly body. It would also rule out any unembodied (pre-mortal) or disembodied (post-mortal) spirits. Moses and Elijah, who were translated and possessed tangible bodies, gave their priesthood keys to Peter, James, and John on the

---

[5]Musser, *Hidden Revelations*, p. 30.

[6]*A Priesthood Issue*, p. 25.

[7]Ibid., pp. 9-15.

[8]Joseph Fielding Smith, *Teachings of the Prophet Joseph Smith* (Salt Lake City: Deseret News Press, 1938), pp. 180-181. Also quoted in *A Priesthood Issue*, p. 7.

Mount of Transfiguration,[9] and this illustrates that means are available to the Lord for the performance of such ordinances. Thus it is not necessary for Heavenly Father himself to personally come to earth to perform a priesthood ordination. Indeed, it would be inconsistent if God himself should overstep his servants, which would in effect nullify the keys he has given them.

When Joseph Smith received the Melchizedek Priesthood, it was under the hands of the resurrected Peter, James, and John, and he received the keys from "divers angels." The Twelve Apostles received all the keys of the kingdom from Joseph Smith, not under the hands of God or Christ personally. The Lord promised Joseph: "The keys of this kingdom shall never be taken from you, while thou art in the world, neither in the world to come; nevertheless, through *you* shall the oracles be given to another, yea, even unto the *church*."[10] The Lord would not have stated to Joseph that the oracles would be given "through you" to another, if these keys could be given only under the hands of God himself personally.

The Lord said to Edward Partridge: "I will lay my hand upon you by the hand of my servant Sidney Rigdon."[11] Thus, whether it is God's personal act or the act of his representative, it is the same.

In the Book of Revelation it is recorded that an angel spoke to John saying, "Behold, I come quickly: blessed is he that keepeth the sayings . . . of this book." When John heard these things, he "fell down to worship before the feet of the angel." The angel said, "See thou do it not: for I am thy fellowservant, and of thy brethren the prophets, and of them which keep the sayings of this book: worship God." Then, speaking again in the first person, *as though he were God,* the angel concluded: "I am Alpha and Omega, the beginning and the end, the first and the last."[12] Finally, the Lord stated in his preface to the Doctrine and Covenants, "Whether by mine own

[9]See Smith, *Teachings,* p. 158. Also see McConkie, *Mormon Doctrine,* p. 805.
[10]D&C 90:3-4. (Italics added.)
[11]Ibid., 36:2.
[12]Revelation 22:7-13.

voice or by the voice of my servants, it is the same."[13] This is in harmony with the concept that God works out his purposes only through the active participation of man.

The Lord revealed knowledge, priesthood and keys as stated before: "Line upon line, precept upon precept; here a little, and there a little;"[14] until they had all been conferred upon men, and for every priesthood, power, or key that was given, there were witnesses so that all the world could know of it. Even though the Prophet Joseph Smith had received the Melchizedek Priesthood from Peter, James, and John, he did not at that time possess all the keys necessary to build up the kingdom. Thus, it is not surprising that the original Twelve in this dispensation did not receive all the keys of the priesthood at once. The Prophet could not give them, for he did not yet possess them.

The procedure is the same today. A man must have the priesthood conferred upon him; afterward he is set apart or ordained to an office and is given all the keys pertaining to that office and calling. Since these early times, each man who is ordained to the apostolic calling receives *all* the keys, but this was not possible at the time of the ordination of the original Twelve.

This delay between the ordination of the original Twelve Apostles and the bestowal of the keys in no way justifies the claim that there are two orders of apostles. Elder Pratt (quoted before) stated, "The fact is, when the order of the kingdom is fully established, the Twelve are the only general officers of the church whose jurisdiction is *universal*."[15] The use of the word *universal* implies that the Twelve direct *all* the affairs of the priesthood and the kingdom.

This claim was substantiated by Brigham Young when he spoke to the Saints in 1844, following the death of Joseph Smith, regarding the claim of the Twelve to lead the Church in the absence of the First Presidency: "I say unto you that the

---

[13]D&C 1:38.
[14]Ibid., 128:21.
[15]*Millennial Star,* 5(1845):152.

Quorum of the Twelve have the keys of the kingdom of God in *all* the world: ... this is true, so help me God."[16]

The Patriarch and the Church

The Fundamentalists postulate that the office of patriarch is higher than the office of President of the Church and that a man holding such an office, acting as Presiding Patriarch, presides over and directs the labors of the First Presidency and the Twelve.[17] As proof of this claim, they cite Doctrine and Covenants 124:124:

> First, I give unto you Hyrum Smith to be a patriarch unto you, to hold the sealing blessings of my church, even the Holy Spirit of promise, whereby ye are sealed up unto the day of redemption, that ye may not fall notwithstanding the hour of temptation that may come upon you.

However, the Lord indicated, "It is the duty of the Twelve, in all large branches of the church, to ordain evangelical ministers [patriarchs], as they shall be designated unto them by revelation."[18] The patriarch derives his appointment (keys) from the Twelve, therefore he cannot be greater than the Twelve.

The question of the nature of the office of patriarch arose as early as 1845. Elder John Taylor, at that time an apostle and editor of the Nauvoo *Times and Seasons*, addressed this problem. We quote his editorial in total as it completely clarified this priesthood office in an official Church statement.

> Since the publication of the last *Times and Seasons,* we have frequently been interrogated about the meaning of some remarks made by Eld. Wm. Smith in an article headed patriarchal, and also concerning some expressions in the editorial connected therewith; and as the nature of the office of Patriarch does not seem to be fully understood, we thought a little explanation on this point might not be amiss.

16Smith, *History of the Church,* 7:233. (Italics added.)

17*A Priesthood Issue,* p. 7. Also quoted in LeBaron, *Priesthood Expounded,* pp. 38-40, 44, 46, 51-55.

18D&C 107:39.

So far as the editorial is concerned it was written rather hastily by our Junior Editor, W. W. Phelps, and did not come under our notice until after it was published. There are some expressions contained in it, which might have been worded better and have rendered it less subject to criticism; but he assures us that no such intention was intended to be conveyed as that which is conceived by some. And concerning Brother Wm. Smith, we are better acquainted with him, and with his views, than to believe that he intended to convey any such idea as the one which some persons would put upon, or gather from his sayings.

In regard to the office of Patriarch, William Smith has been ordained Patriarch *to* the church; but he is not the only Patriarch, but would act as a senior Patriarch, holding the keys of that priesthood; and his labors would be more especially connected with the church in *Zion;* and he would take the lead, priority, or presidency of the Patriarchal office in this place; and in this capacity, if there should be a council of Patriarchs, he as a matter of course would preside by right of office — but every legally ordained Patriarch has the same right to bless that he has, and their administrations are just as legal as his are. Every ordinance that is administered by a legal administrator, is legal. A priest has just as much right to baptize a person for the remission of sins as an elder, a high priest, or an apostle; but he cannot lay on hands for the gift of the Holy Ghost, because he does not possess the authority to do it; but an elder does, and an elder's administration would be just as legal as the administration of any of the beforementioned persons, or as that of the president of the church.

Every father, after he has received his patriarchal blessing, is a Patriarch to his own family, and has the right to confer patriarchal blessings upon his family: which blessings will be just as legal as those conferred by any Patriarch of the church; in fact, it is his right; and a Patriarch in blessing his children, can only bless as his mouthpiece.

A Patriarch to the church is appointed to bless those who are orphans, or have no father in the church to bless them. Not, as stated inadvertently in the editorial above alluded to, "to bless all, and such as have not a father to do it," for this he could not do, where the church is so extensive; the burden would be too onerous; hence other Patriarchs have been ordained, both in this country and in England, to assist the Patriarch to the church, and hence the provision made in the Doctrine and Covenants: "It is the duty of the Twelve, in *all* large branches of the church, to ordain *evangelical ministers* [patriarchs], as they shall be designated unto them by revelation." And should any of those patriarchs remove here, they have just as much right to administer in their patriarchal office under the direction of the patriarch to the church, as an elder or priest would, who should remove from one of the branches to this place, under the direction of the presidency. Brother William Smith, however, "holds the keys of the patriarchal blessings upon the heads of all my people," and would of necessity have the seniority, and of course the priority and presidency; yet it would be left for those who wished to be administered to, to make their choice; just as much as it would for a candidate for baptism to choose who should administer to him.

The above is the true doctrine of the church in regard to this matter, and we speak of it for the information of the brethren at large, lest those who may have received their patriarchal blessings from other sources, or from their fathers, might be tempted to think they were of no avail, and also to set at rest this agitated question.

We now proceed to answer some of the remarks which we have heard:

We have been asked, "Does not patriarch over the whole church" place Brother William Smith at the head of the whole church as president?

Ans. No. Brother William is not patriarch *over* the *whole* church, but patriarch to the church, and as such he was ordained. The expression "over the whole church," is a mistake made by W. W. Phelps. He is patriarch to The Church of Jesus Christ of Latter-day Saints. The Twelve are commanded to ordain evangelical ministers in all large branches of the church abroad, and who has charge over them? The patriarch? No. Those who ordained them. And to whom is committed the power and authority to regulate all the affairs of the churches abroad? And who has the charge of the whole priesthood here? Answer. The presidency of the church, and not the patriarch.

But does not the Doctrine and Covenants say:

"First, I give unto you Hyrum Smith to be a Patriarch unto you to hold the sealing blessings of my church, even the Holy Spirit of promise, whereby ye are sealed up unto the day of redemption, that ye may not fall."

Yes, but that is in regard to seniority not in regard to authority in priesthood, for it immediately follows, "I give unto you my servant Joseph to be a *presiding elder* over *all* my church." In page 110, D.C., we read "the duty of president of the office of the high priesthood is to preside over the whole church, and to be like unto Moses." And from this it is evident that the president of the church, not the patriarch, is appointed by God to preside.

But does not the Patriarch stand in the same relationship to the church as Adam did to his family, and as Abraham and Jacob did to theirs? No. This is another mistake which is made by our junior, and one that may be very easily made inadvertently. Adam was the *natural* father of his posterity, who were his family and over whom he presided as patriarch, prophet, priest, and king. Both Abraham and Jacob stood in the same relationship to their families. But not so with Father Joseph Smith, Hyrum Smith, or William Smith. They were not the natural fathers of the church, and could not stand in the same capacity as Adam, Abraham or Jacob; but inasmuch as there had been none to bless for generations past, according to the ancient order, they were ordained and set apart for the purpose of conferring patriarchal blessings, to hold the keys of this priesthood, and unlock the door, that had long been closed upon the human family: that blessings might again be conferred according to the ancient order, and those who were orphans, or had no father to bless them, might receive it through a patriarch who should act as proxy for their father, and that fathers might again be enabled to act as patriarchs to their families, and bless their children. For like all other ordinances in the church, this had been neglected and must needs be restored. But Father Joseph Smith was not president of the church, nor the president's council. Nor was Hyrum Smith either president or president's council. He was once council, but when he was ordained patriarch he gave it up and another was ordained in his stead, (Wm. Law) and in all probability if Br. William magnifies his calling, he will not be able henceforth to attend to the duties of an apostle; but officiate in the same capacity in regard to blessings as his brother Hyrum did. Not as president of the church, but as patriarch to it.

The president of the church presides over all patriarchs, presidents, and councils of the church; and the presidency does not depend so much upon genealogy as upon calling, order, and seniority. James and Joses were the brothers of Jesus, and John was his beloved disciple, yet Peter held the keys and presided over all the Church. Br. William was in the quorum of the Twelve yet he was not president of the Twelve during his brother's lifetime, nor since; and if being ordained a patriarch would make him president of the church, it would have made Father Joseph Smith and Hyrum Smith presidents over the church instead of Joseph.

Br. William understands the matter, and were it not for the folly of some men there would be no necessity for these remarks.

A Patriarch is what is termed in scripture an evangelist, and Br. William acts in that capacity, and God placed in the church "*first* apostles," not first evangelists, but the president stands in the

> same relationship to the church as Moses did to the children of Israel, according to the revelations.
>
> Again, who ordained Father Smith to the office of patriarch? His son Joseph, and Father Smith ordained Hyrum, and the twelve (of whom Br. William is one) ordained him. Who are appointed to ordain evangelical ministers? [It is the duty of the Twelve, in all large branches of the church, to ordain evangelical ministers, as they shall be designated unto them by revelation.] Can a stream rise higher than its fountain? No . . . says Paul, "Verily the less is blessed of the better."
>
> We think that everyone will see that Br. William Smith's patriarchal office will not exalt him higher in regard to priesthood than he was before, as one of the Twelve; but will rather change the nature of his office.
>
> But will it take anything from his priesthood? it may be asked. No. You cannot take any man's priesthood away without transgression. Br. William will still retain the same power, priesthood, and authority that he did before, and yet will hold in connection with that the patriarchal office and the keys of that priesthood, and as one of the Twelve must maintain his dignity as one of the presidents of the church, of whom President Brigham Young is the president and head, and presides over all patriarchs, presidents, and councils of the church.[19]

The Perfect Order

On Sunday, 16 July 1843, Joseph Smith gave a sermon in which he announced his intention to "not prophesy any more, and proposed Hyrum to hold the office of Prophet to the Church, as it was his birthright, . . . that I might be a Priest of the Most High God."[20] Hyrum had been previously ordained to the office of Associate President.[21] Joseph explained that "the office of Associate President is to assist in presiding over the whole church, and to officiate in the absence of the president." He was also to "hold the keys of the kingdom of heaven or the church militant."[22] Willard Richards reported this sermon in a letter to Brigham Young in which he added that

[19]*The Times and Seasons,* 6 vols. (Nauvoo, Illinois: 1839-1846), 6:920-922.

[20]Smith, *History of the Church,* 5:510.

[21]D&C 124:94-95.

[22]*Manuscript History of the Church,* Book A, 1, quoted in Hyrum L. Andrus, *Doctrines of the Kingdom* (Salt Lake City: Bookcraft, 1973), p. 554-555.

Joseph "did not tell them he was going to be a priest now, or a king by and by."[23]

These statements were interpreted by members of the Church that Joseph was going to resign,[24] but he concluded that they did not understand the Melchizedek Priesthood.[25] He further stated:

> Have we not learned the Priesthood after the order of Melchizedek, which includes both Prophets, Priests and Kings: see Rev. 1 Chap., 6th v., and I will advance your Prophet to a Priest, and then to a King — not to the Kingdoms of this earth, but of the Most High God.[26]

It appears that Joseph visualized a more perfect order of things where he would take his place as the head in a patriarchal society and Hyrum would act as President of the Church.[27] A precedent for this is seen among the Nephites when Mosiah reigned as priest and king over the people and appointed Alma to organize "churches throughout all the land of Zarahemla" and to preside "over the church."[28] In this arrangement Mosiah had political power over the people and reigned as a judge, priest, and king over them while Alma directed the Church.

These incidents have been cited by the Fundamentalists as proof for their assertion that a man holding the appropriate keys of the priesthood may be superior to and act independent of the Church.[29] This is an unwarranted interpretation of these events, however, since the Lord has indicated that the keys of the priesthood reside in their fulness in only one man at a time upon the earth,[30] and that man is President of the High Priesthood and is by definition President of the Church.[31]

---

[23]Smith, *History of the Church,* 5:512.

[24]Smith, *Teachings,* p. 318.

[25]Smith, *History of the Church,* 5:517-518.

[26]Smith, *Teachings,* p. 318.

[27]Andrus, *Doctrines,* p. 554-557.

[28]Mosiah 25:19; 26:8.

[29]Lynn L. Bishop and Steven L. Bishop, *The Keys of the Priesthood Illustrated* (Draper, Utah: Review and Preview Publishers, 1971), pp. 79-85.

[30]D&C 132:7.

[31]Ibid., 107:91-92.

The president may call another man to be an *associate* president and or a prophet to the Church as Joseph did in the case of Hyrum or as Mosiah did in the case of Alma. This is similar to what might happen if the President of the Church became incapacitated by ill health; then his counselor, who is addressed as "president," would "officiate in the absence of the president" and would act as "president militant" until the President recovered. If he died, the Quorum of the First Presidency would be dissolved and the leadership would revert back to the Twelve.[32] But there is no way that a man can act superior to and independent of the Church or of the Church counsels.[33]

The only way that Joseph could assume the role of king, "but not of the kingdoms of the earth," is in relation to his own posterity in the patriarchal order. Because he is not literally the father of the members of the Church, he cannot be patriarch in the sense that Adam was to his children.[34] However, Joseph by divine appointment held the keys of this dispensation and will continue to hold them whether in this life or the next. In this sense he is the great patriarch of the dispensation of the fulness of times and all apostles, prophets, and indeed all who hold the priesthood in this dispensation must recognize his position in standing over them and must ultimately, in the eternities, report their stewardship to him.

Further, by divine right and by the right of physical lineage[35] Joseph could rule as king in a political sense over all the earth. But he would never have attempted to do that except perhaps in a provisional sense, in anticipation of the perfect order, because the Church members were not prepared. Rather, the mission of the Church is to prepare a people ready to receive their king who will be Christ the Lord at his second coming.

---

[32]Smith, *History of the Church,* 7:233.
[33]D&C 107:81-82.
[34]See John Taylor's editorial on the office of patriarch, this chapter.
[35]2 Nephi 3:7, 15; also Smith, *History of the Church,* 5:510.

Conclusion

The Fundamentalists postulate that there are special priesthood orders unknown to the Church, in order to substantiate their claims to secret priesthood provisions upon which they are founded. It has already been shown that the priesthood and the Church are one and the same; however, these claims have been considered in this chapter and shown to be inconsistent with the actions and teachings of the Prophet Joseph and his associates. These doctrines reveal, on the part of the Fundamentalists, an attempt to substantiate their premise of secret priesthood provisions.

Chapter Eight

Prophetic Revelation

Introduction

The premise upon which the Fundamentalists base their actions has been considered in detail in the previous chapters. This premise of alleged special priesthood provisions given in secret provides a basis for authority going back to Joseph Smith for priesthood action independent of The Church of Jesus Christ of Latter-day Saints.

The objective of this chapter is to consider the true nature of prophetic revelation and contrast this with the Fundamentalist's secret priesthood provisions. The Church of Jesus Christ of Latter-day Saints is based upon prophetic revelation or, as stated before, "that kind of revelation that comes only through the living prophets of God."

The Prophets

The ancient Greeks were an example of an enlightened race of people who thought and spoke wisely on almost every subject. There is hardly an idea or human experience that they failed to inquire into. For example, Claudius Ptolemaeus, an Alexandrian Egyptian of great theoretical capabilities, created the first complete scientific astronomical system to explain the movement of the planets, which system was based upon the mathematics of another great Greek thinker, Euclid.

However, one only has to examine the religion of the Greeks to see how they failed to find the true nature of deity. Paul, an apostle and prophet, recognized this when he preached in Athens and called attention to an altar the Greeks had erected on Mars Hill, with the inscription, "To the unknown god," and stated, "Him I declare unto you."[1]

The Greeks lacked the gift of a singular kind of men: Holy men upon whom the gift of God descends. Justin Martyr, an early Christian apologist, called attention to the advantage of the Christian religion compared with that of the Pagans when he stated, "Neither by nature nor by human skill is it possible for men to know such high and holy things; but only by a gift that descends from above upon holy men from time to time." He states further that these men are called prophets, a type of person entirely unknown to the heathen world.[2]

The primitive Church gloried in the fact that it possessed prophets, and it argued that God made himself known through them. When the prophets were no longer present, the Church experienced an overpowering sense of loss. How the Church grieved the loss of Peter; no longer would they hear his intimate remembrances of Jesus, "for with his death a priceless treasure of such memories perished from the earth."[3]

The true Church must always have living prophets. It is not enough to have the words of the prophets of old preserved in holy writ. This is illustrated in the words of Brigham Young:

> When revelations are given through an individual appointed to receive them, they are given to the understanding of the people. These revelations, after a lapse of years, become mystified to those who were not personally acquainted with the circumstances at the time they were given.[4]

But, *living* prophets have always been unwelcome in the world. It is far easier to honor the dead prophet. He is a price-

[1]Acts 17:23.

[2]Nibley, *World and Prophets,* p. 3.

[3]Edgar J. Goodspeed, *An Introduction to the New Testament* (Chicago: University of Chicago, 1937), p. 133.

[4]*Journal of Discourses,* 3:333. Brigham Young also stated: "Do you know what distance and age accomplish? They produce in people the most reverential awe that can be imagined." (Ibid., p. 335.)

less tradition and spiritual heritage. But the living prophet, a plain man whose human weaknesses are all too evident to his contemporaries, is met with derision. As the Jews who spoke of Jesus, saying, "We know that God spoke unto Moses: as for this fellow, we know not from whence he is,"[5] we find today that the living prophets are hard to accept.

> Here we have something in the nature of a general principle. The rejection of the living prophets and the veneration of dead ones is not a folly limited to one nation or to one generation. It meets us throughout the long history of Israel as a sort of standard procedure.[6]

It is easy to venerate Joseph, Hyrum, Brigham, and the early Church leaders; but to ask men to believe that God speaks to the prophet and president of their own day is a test some cannot pass. The humiliating task of taking instruction from the living prophet of God who has stood as the leader of His church on earth has been too difficult for the Fundamentalists since the days of the Manifesto in 1890, for they have declared that he has received no revelation and has not been properly called.[7]

Those who claim to venerate and build their religion upon the revelations given to prophets now dead are free to interpret them any way they choose, since a dead prophet cannot correct them or call them to repentance. If they had lived in the days of the prophets they now claim to venerate, they would most likely have chafed under the loss of that freedom, and rejected them also. The teachings of the dead prophets provide the substance to reinforce the fabric of their own philosophy upon which they are truly built.

Prophets and Scripture

The scripture was defined by Peter as the history of God's revelations when he said, "Knowing this first, that no prophecy of the scripture is of any private interpretation. For the

[5]John 9:29.
[6]Nibley, *World and Prophets,* p. 6.
[7]*A Priesthood Issue,* pp. 23-24.

prophecy came not in old time by the will of man: but holy men of God spake as they were moved by the Holy Ghost."[8]

The Lord said, "Search the scriptures; for . . . they are they which testify of me."[9] And the Jews in reply said, in effect, "We have the scriptures so we don't need you." But he answered, in effect, "If you believed the scriptures you would believe me."[10]

It is significant that when Jesus appeared to his apostles as the glorified, resurrected Lord, he opened to them the scriptures: "Then opened he their understanding, that they might understand the scriptures."[11] Also, when the Lord and other glorious messengers appeared to Joseph Smith, they also explained the scriptures. This is a powerful recommendation of the scriptures and it signifies their value. However, it is also a powerful demonstration that the scriptures cannot stand alone; even the apostles could not understand the full significance of the scriptures until "their understanding was opened" by their divine Teacher.

In reading the scriptures we must always have an interpreter, but who will qualify for the task? Calvin maintained that "the true church only exists when the pure word is preached."[12] But those who accepted this premise were unable to agree on what the *pure* word was and, as a result, a multitude of sects sprang into being during the reformation, each getting different meanings from the holy writings.

In the end, only a man who speaks by the Spirit can make his way through the maze that is the scriptures. "Without a living prophet, the scripture is indeed what the medieval church called it: a mystery."[13]

These comments apply to what we refer to as the standard works, including modern scripture as well as the written words of dead prophets of our own dispensation. The words of Joseph,

[8] 2 Peter 1:19-20.
[9] John 5:39.
[10] Mark 12:24; John 7:38, 42.
[11] Luke 24:45.
[12] Niesel, *Theology of Calvin,* pp. 194-197.
[13] Nibley, *World and Prophets,* p. 188.

Brigham, and the other early leaders, as recorded in scripture, the *Journal of Discourses,* and other writings that come down to us are of great value, but without living prophets to interpret, they are a mystery.

The living Prophet controls the ministrations of the priesthood for the benefit of mankind. As a result, the believing receive the Holy Ghost by the laying on of hands to enable them to understand the scriptures, as they search them, in harmony with the "holy men of God," living or dead, who speak as they are "moved upon by the Holy Ghost."

We may rightly consider these writings and scriptures as the history of other men's revelations, given at other times, under other circumstances. They are of value to us in at least three ways: they may contain universal truths that apply to men in all ages, they reveal to us God's purposes being fulfilled through people in time, and they apply as they are reaffirmed by the living prophets.

Orson Pratt expressed these thoughts in the following way:

> All of these inspired writings are considered valuable, because they contain, not a different gospel or law, but different items of revelation which were once adapted to the different circumstances of individuals and churches to whom they were given. These ever-varying items of revelation are valuable, not as a law or rule for the church in these days, but as matters of history. . . .
>
> The history of God's revelations, ever varying to suit circumstances, is an encouragement for the Saints in the nineteenth century to seek after new revelations, like the ancients, which shall be adapted to the ever-varying and innumerable circumstances with which they may be surrounded . . . . The history of other men's revelations, callings, and missions, would be of no more advantage to us than the history of a good dinner would be to a hungry man, or the history of the miraculous deliverance of the three Hebrew children from the fiery furnace would be to a man perishing in the flames. Callings and missions in the nineteenth century require new revelations as much as in the first century. The history of others' callings, missions and duties, under certain circumstances gives no knowledge of our callings, missions and duties under different circumstances. . . .

> "Man shall not live by bread alone, but by every word of God." This cannot mean every word which God has spoken in different ages; for it would be impossible to live by all the words of God spoken to Noah — to Abraham — to Moses — to the prophets and to the apostles. Thousands of words which God has given could be obeyed only by the very individuals to whom they were given. No other person could obey them. . . . When new revelations or laws are given for the benefit of a church or people, they are generally communicated through the prophets or other inspired officers of the Church. . . . The man who does not believe in continued revelation among the people of God, is already deceived and has not the religion of the Bible. By rejecting new revelation, he rejects one of the great fundamental principles by which the people of God in all ages are clearly distinguished from every other people.[14]

No man can learn what his calling is by studying the history of other men's callings, and that is in part what the scripture is—the history of other men's callings.

It is important to distinguish between revelation through a living prophet and scripture contained in the canon. Many revelations received by the prophets were never written; some, though written, were never compiled into the standard works. For example, the *History of the Church* contains revelations to Reynolds Cahoon, Frederick G. Williams, and to the Twelve that have not been included in the Doctrine and Covenants.[15]

When living prophets of God make official Church policy statements, we do not demand that they write a "thus saith the Lord" statement in King James English before we accept it as the word of the Lord to us. Nearly every day of his life the Prophet Joseph Smith used the phrase *thus saith the Lord*.[16] However, those who succeeded him in the office of president,

---

[14]Pratt, *Orson Pratt's Works,* pp. 66-68.

[15]Smith, *History of the Church,* 2:299-300.

[16]Wilford Woodruff made the following remarks at a stake conference: "Read the life of Brigham Young and you can hardly find a revelation that he had wherein he said 'thus saith the Lord' but the Holy Ghost was with him; he taught by inspiration and by revelation; but with one exception he did not give these revelations in the form that Joseph did; for they were not written and given as revelations and commandments to the church in the words and name of the Savior. Joseph said, 'thus saith the Lord' almost every day of his life, in laying the foundation of this work. But those who followed him have not deemed it always necessary to say 'thus saith the Lord' yet they have lead the people by the power of the Holy Ghost." Wilford Woodruff, *Deseret Evening News,* 7 November 1891.

prophet, seer and revelator did not necessarily do so; yet they led the Church by inspiration and revelation. Brigham Young, for example, was a master of men. When he planned a task, he could find the right man to do it. He purged the Church of apostates and established the remnant of Israel in the Rocky Mountains, but he made few new written revelations. He stated to the people that they had had "the revelations of Jesus Christ poured upon you like water on the ground," but they complained, saying, "Why do you not write them, brother Brigham?"[17]

The value of the living prophets compared with the scripture is illustrated by President Wilford Woodruff, who related an instance in Church history when one of the brethren stated:

> "You have got the word of God before you here in the Bible, Book of Mormon, and Doctrine and Covenants; you have the written word of God, and you who give revelations should give revelations according to those books, as what is written in these books is the word of God. We should confine ourselves to them."

At this Prophet Joseph Smith turned to President Brigham Young and said:

> "Brother Brigham I want you to take the stand and tell us your views with regard to the living oracles and the written word of God." Brother Brigham took the stand, and he took the Bible, and laid it down; he took the Book of Mormon, and laid it down, and he took the Book of Doctrine and Covenants, and laid it down before him, and he said, "There is the written word of God to us, concerning the work of God from the beginning of the world, almost, to our day. And now," said he, "when compared with the living oracles, those books are nothing to me; those books do not convey the word of God direct to us now, as do the words of a Prophet or a man bearing the holy Priesthood to our day and generation. I would rather have the living oracles than all the writing in the books." That was the course he pursued. When he was through, Brother Joseph said to the congregation: "Brother Brigham has told you the word of the Lord and he has told you the truth."[18]

---

[17]*Journal of Discourses,* 3:337.

[18]Wilford Woodruff in *Conference Report of The Church of Jesus Christ of Latter-day Saints,* October 1897, pp. 18-19.

Conclusion

The saints of God in all ages are founded, not upon scripture, the history of God's revelations to other people under other circumstances, nor upon secret priesthood provisions, but upon living prophets.

The Lord defined his church as The Church of Jesus Christ of Latter-day Saints and he has given the First Presidency and Quorum of the Twelve all the keys of the kingdom. The true saints are founded upon revelation through these apostles and prophets.

From time to time, throughout the entire history of Israel, ancient and modern, there have been those who could not accept the leadership of God's prophets. They have based their actions on their private interpretations of the sayings of dead men. Their movements have flourished occasionally, but have been marked by division and subdivision.

Chapter Nine

False Prophets

Introduction

The Church of Jesus Christ is a church of prophets; however, there are many independent groups that are in reality imitation churches. They are cheap substitutes for the real thing. Acting in the name of Christ is not enough, for the Lord said: "Many will say to me in that day, Lord, Lord, have we not prophesied in thy name, and in thy name have cast out devils? and in thy name done many wonderful works?" And he will say, "I never knew you: depart from me, ye that work iniquity."[1]

To make it appear real, the two things needed by an imitation church are priesthood claims and spiritual confirmation of those claims. We have considered the claims to priesthood authority put forward by the various Fundamentalist cult groups in previous chapters. Here we will consider claims of mystic or spiritual confirmation.

Prophecy

Hugh Nibley defines a false prophet thus:

> One who usurps the prerogatives and authority which by right belong only to a prophet of God. The false prophet need not claim to be a prophet . . . anyone, in a word, who puts his own knowledge [or priesthood powers] above or on a level with revelation from

[1]Matthew 7:22-23.

> heaven is a false prophet. . . . A pseudo-prophet is one to whom foolish people accord the obedience and attention due only a true prophet, whether he or they actually take him for a prophet or not.[2]

The greatest spiritual manifestation of priesthood and prophetic powers is the gift of prophecy or, as Paul stated, "Greater is *he* that prophesieth."[3] The leaders of cult groups attempt to demonstrate *their* priesthood powers by issuing profound prophecies.

We have seen that the second-century Gnostics attempted to startle the world by issuing sensational prophecies. They proclaimed that a general war would follow the death of the Lady Maximilla. When this failed, they fell back on mysticism which was deep and mysterious enough to satisfy them as a substitute for prophetic revelation.[4]

The LeBaronite cultists are reputed to have issued a prophecy that their prophet and president, Joel LeBaron, would be the final prophet of the age, since the Christ would come while he was yet alive. This is a startling and apocalyptical proclamation. However, intercult feuding led to his violent death by apparent murder on 28 August 1972 in Mexico.[5]

The testimony of Lorin C. Woolley of the "Provision of 1886" also contains a startling prophecy:

> . . . that in the time of the seventh President of this Church, the church would go into *bondage both temporally and spiritually* and in that day [the day of bondage] the one mighty and strong spoken of in the 85th section of the Doctrine and Covenants would come.[6]

This false prophecy of Woolley's, given in 1929 just after he had been excommunicated as a result of President Heber J. Grant's purge of cultists from the Church, appears to be a form of retaliation against President Grant. As Joseph W. Musser, a confidant of Woolley, explained:

---

[2]Nibley, *World and Prophets,* p. 230, 231.
[3]1 Corinthians 14:5. (Italics added.)
[4]Refer to the section on Gnostics, chapter 2.
[5]*Salt Lake Tribune,* 205(September 7, 1972):146, B4.
[6]Musser, *Hidden Revelations,* p. 31.

> For years after the Manifesto, the Church took a quiescent attitude toward the principle [of plural marriage]. Not until Heber J. Grant became [the seventh] President of the Church was any move inaugurated to stomp the principle out and prosecute those adhering to it. . . .[7]

Whenever cultists make extravagant claims to priesthood authority, they attempt to back up these claims by issuing prophecies and seeking for various spiritual manifestations.

Spiritual Confirmation

Most religious movements of the world have made claims to some form of spiritual experience. Like ritual and philosophy, spiritual manifestations are used by practitioners of religion everywhere to amaze and convince doubters. The Savior warned, "There shall arise . . . false prophets, and shall shew great signs and wonders; insomuch that, if it were possible, they shall deceive the very elect."[8]

Many types of religious inspiration have been claimed by men through the ages. Two of these are *mysticism* and *spiritualism.* Mysticism is *not* a form of prophetic revelation. Most authorities,

> notably Rudolf Bultmann, argued that the emphasis of the New Testament upon the lordship of God and its conception of the historical revelation are in such complete antithesis to any mystical notions that the mystical language of the biblical writers must be seen as a rejection rather than as an adaptation of the mystical tradition. It certainly is true that the idea of a mystical technique for the attainment of unity with God which figures so prominently in the history of mysticism, is absent from the New Testament and alien to its spirit.[9]

Mysticism is difficult to define, but most authorities agree that it is some kind of ecstatic union with the ultimate reality or deity. Such an experience can be obtained by subjecting the mind and body to a prescribed procedure. The mystic

---

[7]Musser, *Plural Marriage,* p. 6.
[8]Matthew 24:24.
[9]*Encyclopedia Britannica,* 15(1969):1130.

experience must be induced by a long period of dedicated effort and practice and it is wholly an experience of the Alone by the alone and could easily be *self-induced*. The principle characteristic of the mystic experience is its *ineffableness*.[10] That is, the experience is utterly indescribable. Nothing of the experience can be conveyed to others.

"What is important in mystical acts is *something happens*. What is important in prophetic acts is *something is said*."[11] Thus self-induced mystic experiences, which might be ascribed to bodily weakness from excessive fasting, or from use of drugs in religious experiences, or from contemplation and mental exercises produce a *happening* but do not communicate the will of God. By contrast, the whole calling of a prophet is to communicate the will of God to men. He has a message and is a witness, and he tells what he has heard and seen. "On Pentecost, . . . on the Mount of Transfiguration, at the Ascension, always there was a *plurality of witnesses;* always they are surprised by what happens; always definite things are seen and heard."[12] Nothing was self-induced or expected.

Spiritualism is "a system of beliefs and practices having the object of communicating with the asserted spirits of those who died,"[13] and includes phenomena of "physical mediumship" and "mental mediumship." Physical mediumship includes *levitation,* the rising of objects or of the human body in the air without the use of mechanical means of support; and *materialization,* the appearance of the bodies or parts of bodies of dead persons. Mental mediumship refers to the obtaining of messages from the dead and includes the ouija board, tappings, necromancy, and voices. Thus there are many spiritual manifestations that cannot be classified as true prophetic revelation; however, they satisfy a certain type of person as a substitute for revelation and constitute the basis for their "testimony."

---

[10]William James, *Pragmatism* (New York, 1907), p. 151.
[11]Herschel, cited in *Encyclopedia Britannica,* 15(1969):1130.
[12]Nibley, *World and Prophets,* p. 96.
[13]*Encyclopedia Britannica,* 21(1969):42.

The "gifts of the Spirit" are *not* to be classified as either mystic experiences or spiritualism. In the first place, these gifts were never given as converting signs. The Lord said it is a "wicked and adulterous generation [that] seeketh after a sign."[14] Also, the prophet Moroni stated, "Ye receive no witness until after the trial of your faith."[15] In the Doctrine and Covenants the Lord defines the reason for the gifts of the Spirit and we are admonished to "seek ye earnestly the best gifts, always remembering for what they are given . . . not for a sign that they may consume it upon their lusts," but "all these gifts come from God, for the benefit of the children of God."[16] It is wrong to seek these experiences as a means of satisfying our pride or gratifying our feelings of righteousness, or as a sign, but they are given to help individuals work out their stewardship *after* the trial of faith.

Against the mystic or spiritualism experience, the gifts of the Spirit are given for the profit of others (as indicated in verses 12 and 26 of the above-referenced section 46 of the Doctrine and Covenants), to convey knowledge (verses 13 through 18), and to further the work of the Lord (verses 19 through 25).

The testimony of Lorin C. Woolley concerning the alleged "Priesthood Provision of 1886" contains, in addition to the false prophecy already considered, allusions to nonprophetic spiritualistic experiences. Three times the prophet John Taylor is alleged to have experienced the phenomena of levitation, "his person rising from the floor about a foot or eighteen inches," and "he frequently arose and stood above the floor,"[17] etc. The materialization of the dead Prophet Joseph Smith is also claimed. "Two of us had not met the Prophet Joseph Smith in his mortal lifetime and we—Charles H. Wilkins and myself—were introduced to him and shook hands with him."[18]

---

[14]Matthew 16:4.
[15]Ether 12:6.
[16]D&C 46:8, 9, 26.
[17]Musser, *Hidden Revelations,* pp. 29-31.
[18]Ibid., p. 31.

Conclusion

There are many spiritual experiences that can be obtained by following certain procedures, but they are not revelations from God. Many of these experiences are profound, deep and mysterious enough to satisfy many people as a substitute for true prophetic revelation.

The testimony of Lorin C. Woolley contains evidence of spiritualism or mystic-type experiences. There was never an occasion when the Prophet Joseph Smith resorted to levitation or other spiritual exercises to convert people to his way of thinking. To attribute such methods to President John Taylor is demeaning to his role as a prophet of God.

However, the Fundamentalists, having claimed to have prophetic powers, are compelled to provide spiritual confirmation of this power. Everyday events are given end-of-the-world significance and interpreted as "witnesses" of various actions to be undertaken. Dreams with significant meaning, ministering of [unseen] angels, materializations of dead persons, feelings, and struggles with the adversary are considered testimonies of their priesthood claims.

The cultist's way of life is founded upon his belief in the priesthood powers of his file leader.[19] These powers must be demonstrated over and over to sustain this belief. So-called priesthood keys and powers are evoked to issue prophecies and to bless homes, cars, and other objects. Three-day (or longer) fasts that usually terminate with a new witness are common. Thus, revelation from God is replaced by mysticism and spiritualism.

[19]Those who reject the living prophets and resort to the Fundamentalist groups are often unable to find the security they seek. They jump "from the frying pan into the fire by following some group that might be a little better versed in the scriptures" (Pierce, *3½ Years,* p. 39), but after drifting from one group to another, many finally come to consider themselves "Independent," concluding that they are not dependent upon any group or any man for their exaltation. They reject both the Church and the groups because without so doing "we'd be dependent upon some man for our exaltation, and I won't stand still for that one minute. God never guaranteed his leaders; in fact, he said, 'cursed is he that puts his trust in man and maketh flesh his arm.' " Then they base this claim to authority upon direct and individual "contact [with] the light of Christ" or in some cases with the Prophet Joseph Smith who, they say, will come to a man who is worthy and prepared, and give him the authority. Mark J. and Rhea A. Baird, "A Discussion June 1971," *Reminiscences of John W. Woolley and Lorin C. Woolley,* Vol. I, p. 8. (No publishing information imprinted.)

Chapter Ten

Individual Revelation and Prophetic Authority

Introduction

As was pointed out in the previous chapter, there are many spiritual manifestations which are not of God. These manifestations are sometimes produced by false prophets to amaze and convince doubters. Also indicated in previous chapters was the fact that The Church of Jesus Christ of Latter-day Saints is founded upon that type of revelation that comes only through living prophets. The purpose of this chapter is to consider the relationship between individual revelation and prophetic authority, and to set forth the means by which one can avoid being deceived by manifestations that are not of God.

To Know the Truth

The Lord has given a simple test by which anyone may challenge those who may come claiming to have had a vision or who claim authority. This test is given in the Doctrine and Covenants, section 42, verse 11:

> Again, I say unto you, that it shall not be given to any one to go forth to preach my gospel, or to build up my church, except he be ordained by some one who has authority, and it is known to the church that he has authority and has been regularly ordained by the heads of the church.

Also in section 43, verses 5-7:

> And this shall be a law unto you, that ye receive not the teachings of any that shall come before you as revelations or commandments [except "him whom I have appointed unto you"]; and this I give unto you that you may not be deceived, that you may know they are not of me. For verily I say unto you, that he that is ordained of me shall come in at the gate and be ordained as I have told you before, to teach those revelations which you have received and shall receive through him whom I have appointed.

Thus, no one can receive revelation for, or impose callings or requirements upon, another person unless it is in strict accordance with his position and calling in the Church. Revelations of a general nature that apply to the Church as a whole can come only through the head or President of the Church; this is because the kingdom of God is "a house of order, saith the Lord God, and not a house of confusion."[1]

Every member of the Church is entitled to the companionship of the Holy Ghost. The gifts of the Spirit, as outlined in section 46 of the Doctrine and Covenants, are not given as signs, but to help a person work out his stewardship in life and to serve in his calling in the Church, and they are given only after the "trial of faith."

The Holy Ghost often influences us through our emotions. This is illustrated by the two disciples who, after speaking with the resurrected Christ, said, "Did not our heart burn within us, while he talked with us by the way, and while he opened to us the scriptures?"[2] The prophet Alma also described this emotional response to the promptings of the Spirit when he compared the word of the gospel to a seed and said, "And now, behold, because ye have tried the experiment, and planted the seed [in your heart], and it swelleth and sprouteth, and beginneth to grow, ye must needs know that the seed is good."[3] Alma insists that this swelling is real, for he said, "O then, is not this real? I say unto you, Yea."[4]

---

[1]D&C 132:8.
[2]Luke 24:32.
[3]Alma 32:33.
[4]Ibid., 32:35.

When Oliver Cowdery attempted and failed to translate the Book of Mormon, the Lord explained:

> But, behold, I say unto you, that you must study it out in your mind; then you must ask me if it be right, and if it is right I will cause that your bosom shall burn within you; therefore, you shall *feel* that it is right. But if it be not right you shall have no such feelings, but you shall have a stupor of thought that shall cause you to forget the thing which is wrong; therefore, you cannot write that which is sacred save it be given you from me.[5]

The principle, "study it out in your mind," applies to anyone who wishes to be enlightened upon the subject of any problem. God helps him who first helps himself. This emphasizes the importance of studying the scriptures and obtaining the counsel of the living prophets and those constituted authorities who are over us in the Church. Above all, we should find out what the official doctrine and policy of the Church is, remembering that we are founded upon living prophets.

If our "bosom" or "heart" is full of wrong emotions, there will be no place for the Holy Ghost to cause the "swellings" or "burnings." A person whose heart is full of anger, rebellion, fear, lust or any other evil influence is incapable of receiving the ministrations of the Spirit, but is highly susceptible to divisive and deluding spirits.

Follow the Prophets

The harmony and order of the kingdom require that we follow the prophets. The Prophet Joseph Smith, while speaking to the original Twelve Apostles, gave this key:

> O ye Twelve! and all Saints! profit by this important *Key* — that in all your trials, troubles, temptations, afflictions, bonds, imprisonments, and death, see to it, that you do not betray heaven; that you do not betray Jesus Christ; that you do not betray the brethren; that you do not betray the revelations of God, whether in the Bible, Book of Mormon, or Doctrine and Covenants, or any other that ever was or ever will be given and revealed unto man

[5]D&C 9:8-9. (Italics added.)

> in this world or that which is to come. Yea, in all your kicking and flounderings, see to it that you do not this thing, lest innocent blood be found upon your skirts, and you go down to hell. All other sins are not to be compared to sinning against the Holy Ghost, and proving a traitor to the brethren.
>
> I will give you one of the *Keys* of the mysteries of the Kingdom. It is an eternal principle, that has existed with God from all eternity: That man who rises up to condemn others, finding fault with the Church, saying that they are out of the way, while he himself is righteous, then know assuredly, that that man is on the high road to apostasy; and if he does not repent, will apostatize, as God lives.[6]

The Prophet on several occasions indicated that it was important to stay with the Church.

> The writer [Elder Edward Stevenson] heard the Prophet say on a stand at the east end of the Nauvoo Temple, that the time was coming when there would be many dissensions from the church. "But," said he, "I now see the time which I have long desired to see. Let me go where I may, the gospel tree is planted never more to be rooted up, for there are those present who are prepared to carry on the gospel, whatever may become of me." He also said: "I will give you *a key by which you may never be deceived,* if you will observe these facts: where the true church is, there will always be a majority of the saints, and the records and history of the church also."[7]

A similar event was also recorded in the diary of William G. Nelson.

> I have heard the Prophet speak in public on many occasions. In one meeting I heard him say: "I will give you a key that will never rust, — if you will stay with the majority of the Twelve Apostles, and the records of the church, you will never be led astray."[8]

The First Presidency in August 1913 issued a warning to the members of the Church that applies today:

---

[6]Smith, *History of the Church,* 3:385.

[7]Andrew Jenson and Edward Stevenson, *Infancy of the Church* (Salt Lake City, 1889), p. 5.

[8]*Young Woman's Journal,* 17(December 1906):542-543.

To the officers and members of The Church of Jesus Christ of Latter-day Saints:

From the days of Hiram Page (Doc. and Cov., Sec. 28), at different periods there have been manifestations from delusive spirits to members of the Church. Sometimes these have come to men and women who because of transgression became easy prey to the Arch-Deceiver. At other times people who pride themselves on their strict observance of the rules and ordinances and ceremonies of the Church are led astray by false spirits, who exercise an influence so imitative of that which proceeds from a Divine source that even these persons, who think they are "the very elect," find it difficult to discern the essential difference. Satan himself has transformed himself to be apparently "an angel of light."

When visions, dreams, tongues, prophecy, impressions or an extraordinary gift or inspiration convey something out of harmony with the accepted revelations of the Church or contrary to the decisions of its constituted authorities, Latter-day Saints may know that it is not of God, no matter how plausible it may appear. Also, they should understand that directions for the guidance of the Church will come, by revelation, through the head. All faithful members are entitled to the inspiration of the Holy Spirit for themselves, their families, and for those over whom they are appointed and ordained to preside. But anything at discord with that which comes from God through the head of the Church is not to be received as authoritative or reliable. In secular as well as spiritual affairs, Saints may receive Divine guidance and revelation affecting themselves, but this does not convey authority to direct others, and is not to be accepted when contrary to Church covenants, doctrine or discipline, or to known facts, demonstrated truths, or good common sense. No person has the right to induce his fellow members of the Church to engage in speculations or take stock in ventures of any kind on the specious claim of Divine revelation or vision or dream, especially when it is in opposition to the voice of recognized authority, local or general. The Lord's Church "is a house of order." It is not governed by individual gifts or manifestations, but by the order and power of the Holy Priesthood as sustained by the voice and vote of the Church in its appointed conferences.

The history of the Church records many pretended revelations claimed by impostors or zealots who believed in the manifestations they sought to lead other persons to accept, and in every instance, disappointment, sorrow and disaster have resulted therefrom. Financial loss and sometimes utter ruin have followed.[9]

---

[9]Quoted in *Conference Report of The Church of Jesus Christ of Latter-day Saints,* October 1972, pp. 125-126.

Conclusion

Not long after the murder of the cult leader Joel LeBaron, the semi-annual conference of the Church was held in October 1972. At that conference President Harold B. Lee said:

> It is likewise a marvel to us today . . . that some members are so soon removed from those who taught them the gospel and are removed from the true teachings of the gospel of Christ to be led astray into something that corrupts the true doctrines of the gospel of Christ into vicious and wicked practices and performances. These, as have been evidenced by shocking events among some of these splinter groups, have been accursed, as the prophets warned; and they are obviously in the power of that evil one who feeds the gullible with all the sophistries which Satan has employed since the beginning of time.[10]

The true people of God in all ages are founded upon that kind of revelation that comes through living prophets. All that is sacred in history, law and scripture originated from that premise. The Fundamentalist cult groups are founded upon secret priesthood provisions allegedly given to men who left no testimonies of these events as required by the law of witnesses. From this premise have sprung a multitude of splinter groups, error, sin, and even death.

---

[10]Ibid., p. 125.

Chapter Eleven

The Sum Total of It All

The purpose of this concluding chapter is to make explicit the singular fact that should by now be obvious: Plural marriage is not the real issue now, nor was it ever. The real issue is one of priesthood authority.

That the real issue is a question of priesthood authority, even before the Manifesto was given in 1890, is illustrated in the following epistle of the First Presidency published in 1886. It stated that the persecution to which the Church was at that time subjected was a conspiracy to destroy the Church. "While engaged in this nefarious business, they throw dust in the eyes of the nation by making an outcry against polygamy—as if they cared anything about our marriages—in order to conceal and accomplish their deeper design."[1]

Those who opposed the Church feared the power of a unified, monolithic group, but found opposition to polygamy as a convenient handle to oppress the Church. Men like Fredrick T. Dubois were interested in destroying the centralized control of the Church, the priesthood:

> Those of us who understood the situation were not nearly as much opposed to polygamy as we were to the political domination of the church. We realized, however, that we could not make those who did not come actually into contact with it, understand what this political domination meant. We made use of polygamy in con-

---

[1]*Deseret News,* April 14, 1886.

> sequence as our great weapon of offense and to gain recruits to our standard. There was a universal detestation of polygamy, and inasmuch as the Mormons openly defended it we were given a very effective weapon with which to attack.[2]

How effective this weapon was is illustrated in the case of *Davis* v. *Beason,* when the Supreme Court struck down the rights of members of the Church to religious freedom under the Constitution. In this decision, the court upheld an Idaho law which provided that:

> No person who is a bigamist or polygamist, or who teaches, advises, counsels or encourages any person or persons to become bigamists or polygamists, or to commit any other crime defined by law, or to enter into what is known as plural or celestial marriage, or who is a member of any order, organization or association which teaches, advises, counsels or encourages its members or devotees or any other person to commit the crime of bigamy or polygamy, or any other crime defined by law, either as a rite or ceremony of such order, organization or association, or otherwise, is permitted to *vote at* any election, or to *hold* any *position* of honor, trust or *profit* within this territory.[3]

Based on this law, the court denied Davis, who had never practiced polygamy, his rights as a citizen simply because he was a member of the Church.

We have seen that the sealing keys pertain exclusively to the presidency of the Church,[4] and that the Fundamentalists claim special orders of priesthood higher than that of the President of the Church.[5] Thus, the Fundamentalist movement represents a direct rebellion against the priesthood authority of the prophet of God.

Those who would claim that it is their sincere desire to practice plural marriage so that they may obtain the blessings of living that principle—as if they really felt that plural mar-

---

[2]Autobiography of Fredrick T. Dubois, quoted in Hansen, "Metamorphosis," *Dialogue,* 1(Autumn 1966):75.

[3]*U.S. Reports,* Vol. 133, October 1889, (New York and Albany: Banks and Brothers, 1890), p. 333ff, from Gordon C. Thompson, "The Manifesto was a Victory!" *Dialogue,* 6(Spring 1971):42.

[4]See chapter 5.

[5]See chapter 7.

riage was the only significant gospel principle—are using plural marriage to conceal and accomplish their deeper design, which is to rebel against the living prophet of God and usurp authorities that they do not even begin to understand.

The Lord warned against those who pretend to have priesthood when they do not:

> Wherefore, let all men beware how they take my name in their lips — For behold, verily I say, that many there be who are under this condemnation, who use the name of the Lord, and use it in vain, having not authority.[6]

He also warned those who would rebel against the prophet:

> Cursed are all those that shall lift up the heel against mine anointed, saith the Lord, and cry they have sinned when they have not sinned before me, saith the Lord. . . . But those who cry transgression do it because they are the servants of sin, and are the children of disobedience themselves. And those who swear falsely against my servants. . . . Their basket shall not be full, their houses and their barns shall perish, and they themselves shall be despised by those that flattered them. They shall not have right to the priesthood, nor their posterity after them from generation to generation.[7]

We conclude with this statement by President Harold B. Lee:

> I have one other thought I should like to express. Brigham Young was a great defender of the Prophet Joseph Smith. There were Judases in the ranks in that day, just as there were in the Savior's day, and just as we have today, some who are members of the Church who are undercutting us, who are betraying their trusts. We are shocked when we see the places from which some of these things come.
>
> Brigham Young was invited by some of these men who were trying to depose the Prophet Joseph from his position as President of the Church; but they made a mistake by inviting President Brigham Young into their circle. And after he had listened to what

---

[6]D&C 63:61-62.
[7]Ibid., 121:16-18, 20.

their motives were, he said something to this effect: "I want to say something to you men. You cannot destroy the appointment of a prophet of God, but you can cut the thread that binds you to the prophet of God, and sink yourselves to hell.[8]

---

[8]Harold B. Lee in *Conference Report of the Church of Jesus Christ of Latter-day Saints,* October 1972, p. 129.

Index